Revolutionary New Castle

THE STRUGGLE FOR INDEPENDENCE

THEODORE CORBETT

THE History PRESS

Published by The History Press
Charleston, SC 29403
www.historypress.net

Illustrations are courtesy of the author unless otherwise noted.

First published 2012

Manufactured in the United States

ISBN 978.1.60949.524.4

Library of Congress Cataloging-in-Publication Data

Corbett, Theodore, 1941-
Revolutionary New Castle : the struggle for independence / Theodore Corbett.
p. cm.
Includes bibliographical references and index.
ISBN 978-1-60949-524-4
1. New Castle (Del.)--History--18th century. 2. Delaware--History--Revolution, 1775-1783. I. Title.
F174.N5C67 2012
975.1'02--dc23
2012001586

Notice: The information in this book is true and complete to the best of our knowledge. It is offered without guarantee on the part of the author or The History Press. The author and The History Press disclaim all liability in connection with the use of this book.

Contents

Acknowledgements 5
Introduction 7

New Castle in the Era of Revolution 19
Churches in the Independence Movement 31
The Assembly, Courts and Committees 51
What Was It Like to Go to War 57
Howe's Occupation 65
Civil War from Coast to River 71
Fulfilling the Promise of Independence 81
Support for the Federal Constitution, Not the Federalist Party 101

Affirmations 115
Selected Bibliography 119
Index 123
About the Author 128

Acknowledgements

This account of New Castle's role in the Revolution is far from exhaustive. Prose moves too smoothly over topics that are far more complicated than they appear. It is my hope that debate will deepen and continue on these topics, especially those that have not been thoroughly explored.

In 2010, ideas in the introduction of this book first saw light in an exhibit on New Castle's Town Hall sponsored by the New Castle Historical Society. Since then, this endeavor would not have possible without the effort and encouragement of Mike Connelly and the New Castle Historical Society, Kathy McDonough and the Trustees of the Common, Dr. Constance Cooper and the Delaware Historical Society, Cathryn Thomas and the City of New Castle and Special Collections at the University of Delaware Library. Also, my brother, Jim, has always inspired me when it comes to the Revolutionary War. If any book were to be singled out as indispensible in writing this, it would be Liam Riordan's *Many Identities, One Nation*. Most of all, I am thankful for subtle exchanges with my colleague, Herb Pratt, and the livelier discussions I have had with Reverend Nancy Rowland, Jim Meek, Bill Quillen, Victor Clark, Don Reese, Joan Smith, Andrew Lundgren and Charlotte Mitchell-McDowell, affiliates of the History Committee of New Castle Presbyterian Church. I dedicate this book to that committee.

Introduction

The focus here is on those who lived in New Castle and participated in the pre- and post-Revolution years, as well as the actual war. It visualizes the Revolutionary era broadly, as a protest movement in the 1760s and then an era of formal and civil war, as well as in its aftermath the effort to fulfill the promise of the Revolution. In 1797, the Fourth of July was celebrated with a full day of activities in New Castle. It began with a flag raising at sunrise, followed by an oration at the Presbyterian meetinghouse attended by both men and women and then a move to the courthouse, where 140 sat down to a meal attended by the governor and a native son, Gunning Bedford Sr., and four militia companies. Toasts followed all afternoon, and the festivities did not break up until six o'clock at night. It remains to be seen how the Fourth became a pivotal event in New Castle's history.

Today, people enjoy exploring the historic streets and houses of old New Castle. This history can be used as a guide of the places and events of the Revolutionary era. It offers a new perspective for exploring the community that first focuses on civic spaces and then shows us how these spaces came alive during the era. The Courthouse, Market House, Green and Common were already present with their own histories when the momentous events of the Revolutionary era occurred. These spaces were natural backdrops for the citizens of New Castle to gather, express their convictions and use for their own well-being. The exception is the Town Hall, which was erected in 1826 at the end of the era, a sign that the Revolution had prolonged the effort to obtain municipal government. After a brief review

Contemporary map of New Castle. *Courtesy City of New Castle.*

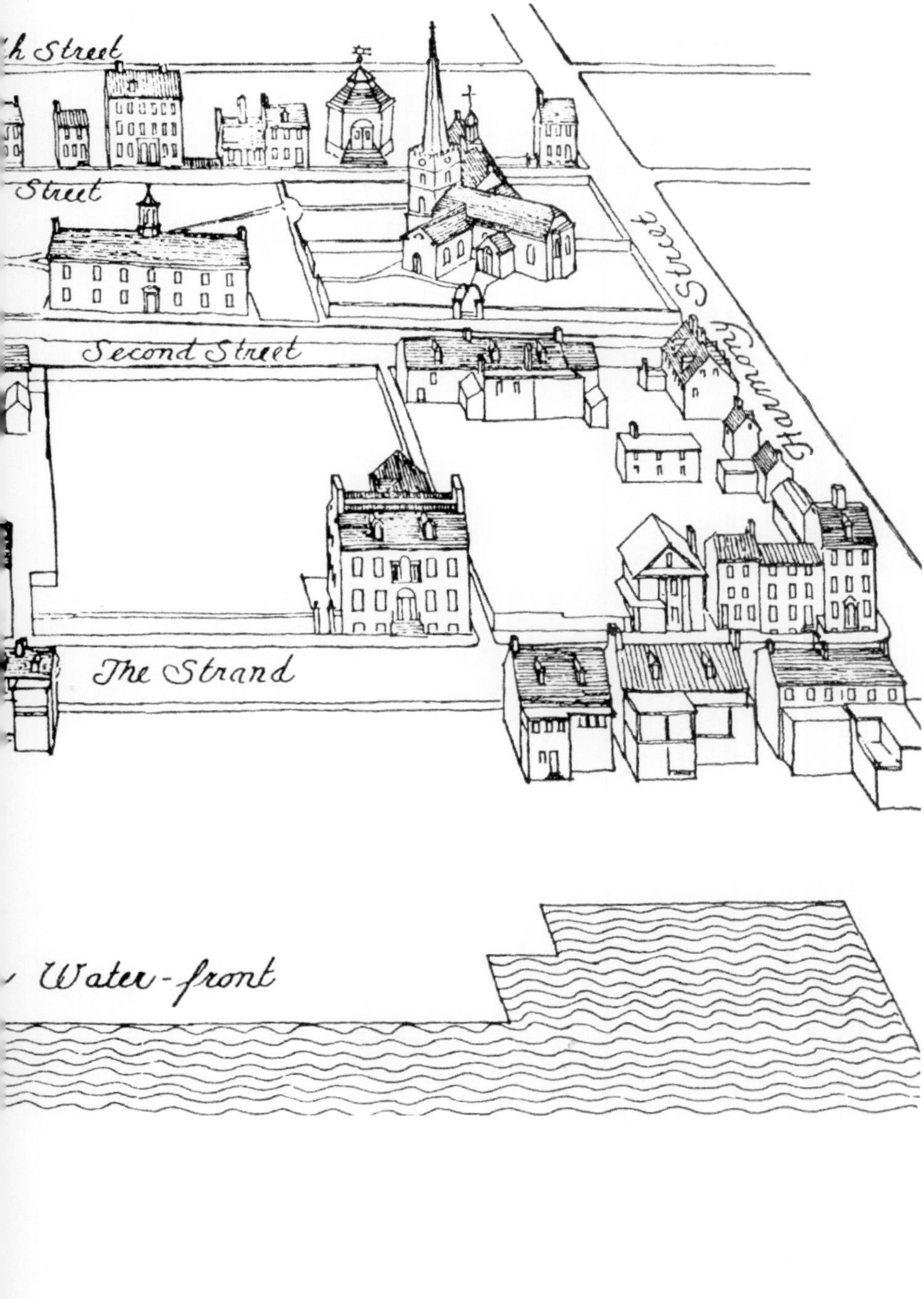

h Street
Street
Second Street
Harmony Street
The Strand
Water-front

of these five existing spaces, we will be oriented and ready to investigate the Revolutionary conflict.

The first space, the Market House, had a protective role, ensuring that New Castle's citizens would have a healthful, abundant and unadulterated supply of perishable food. A European and colonial tradition, public markets were held and regulated by municipalities for the benefit of the community. The market focused on the sale of beef, lamb, pork, fish, dairy products and

Left: Market and Town Hall, 1826. A watercolor by New Castle's Robert Montgomery Bird of the market, extending from the back of the Town Hall; it is the earliest surviving view of both. *Courtesy Robert Bird.*

Below: The Green, established 1655. New Castle's oldest civic space was at first used to keep animals overnight. When the movement for independence came, it was the scene of protest against the tyranny of Parliament.

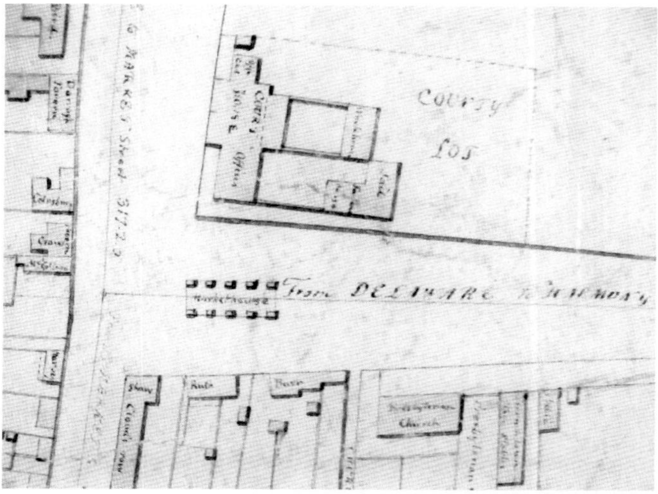

Footprints of market, Courthouse complex and Presbyterian meetinghouse, from an 1805 survey, Benjamin Latrobe and assistants. *Courtesy New Castle Historical Society.*

bread, the perishables that needed to be controlled. A public market was held in New Castle apparently as early as the Dutch occupation in 1655. A formal market was granted a charter by the Lower Counties Assembly in 1740. At first, New Castle held markets on Wednesday and Saturday. In 1806, the state legislature was petitioned, asking that its market days be changed because they were the same as Wilmington's. The only trace today of the New Castle Market House is an eighty-foot-long brick area to the rear of the Town Hall that served as the market's floor.

A market was operating in the midst of Market Street where it converged with Delaware Street in the second half of the eighteenth century. The earliest markets probably did not require permanent structures, with each participant setting up a booth on specific days, probably closing Market Street to traffic. A market house was seen by a visitor in 1759. On June 13, 1772, an act of the Delaware Assembly asserted that the land in the midst of Market Street was owned and managed by the Market Trustees for the public good. The 1805 Latrobe map shows the footprint of a market house on this spot—basically two lines of buttresses that probably supported a segmented roof. Thus a market house was there throughout the entire Revolutionary period.

From 1826, New Castle's existing market could be entered through the central arcade of the Town Hall. A view of that year shows that the existing market stretched eighty feet from the back wall of the Town Hall to the market's gabled end. At this end was a three-sided entranceway with a hipped roof. On either side of the market shed were stalls that were open to the street. The market shed was more of an open pavilion than a closed public structure. It is probable that carts were backed into the stalls and served as booths.

Statue of William Penn. A Quaker, Penn first reached Newcastle on the Delaware in October 1682, taking formal possession of his extensive grant. He is portrayed holding a key, a turf and twig and a container of water, symbols used in the common law ceremony of "livery of seisin."

The nearby Green was the chief civic space in New Castle's center, stretching behind the courthouse between Third and Market Streets and ending at Immanuel Church and the Academy. It was established on a hill, the highest point in the community, although over the years it has been leveled so that today the incline is almost imperceptible. The Green is not to be confused with the Common, which will soon be discussed.

The Green was designated as public land in 1655 during the Dutch period. However, the Dutch only governed for a dozen years, and it is unlikely that they improved the extensive empty space. In the 1670s, the English, who now held the colony in the name of the Duke of York, built a blockhouse on the Green that served as a guardhouse, jail and place of meeting for monthly courts. From 1682, the new English proprietor, William Penn, required green squares in laying out communities in Delaware and Pennsylvania. New Castle's existing green fit into his plans and must have served as pasture for residents' livestock during the evening. In daytime, the animals were probably driven to the extensive pasture in the Common and adjacent areas and then returned each evening for protection and, in the case of cows, to be milked. Effort was made to prevent animals from roaming the streets, especially feisty feral pigs.

Thus the Green began as a messy place in the center of town to protect livestock, especially milk cows, overnight. At the time of the Revolution,

A Southwest View of Immanuel Church and the Academy in the Town of New Castle, Sept. 1822. Handed down in the Janvier family, the view shows a fenced and gated Green, with a post and rail fence at three levels, with the top/fourth level covered with plank. A post and rail gate opens along Delaware Street, and a fancier pointed iron gate is in the rear that serves as the entrance to Immanuel churchyard. A willow and a few fur trees are on the eastern and western edges of the Green. Immanuel's burial yard has trees, but they do not create a landscaped space. *Courtesy New Castle Historical Society.*

it was designated for four uses: public buildings, the Immanuel Church, a school and markets and fairs. These activities involved bits of the space on the edges of the Green that defined the boundaries you see today.

In 1772, the Delaware Assembly established boards of trustees for different sectors of the Green, including, as noted, trustees for public buildings, the Immanuel Church, a school and markets and fairs. At the time of the Revolution, the Green contained a whipping post, a pair of stocks, a hog pen, a signal cannon and a jail. It is also likely that fairs were held semiannually in the extensive space. As the market grew and was held on one portion of the Green, the remaining space began to be called the Public Square.

The Green's greatest moment as a gathering space came on June 29, 1774, when about five hundred people of all classes congregated there to debate the Intolerable Acts that Parliament had used to punish Boston for spearheading the Independence movement. New Castle's mass meeting was one of several coordinated by the Philadelphia Committee of Correspondence and was a sign of New Castle's support for the Revolutionary cause.

After the Revolutionary War, the transition from the utilitarian to the ornamental green was gradual. The Green was called the "Public Square" on architect Benjamin Latrobe's 1805 planning-drainage map of New Castle. It was now the responsibility of the Five Commissioners of the town. Latrobe's accompanying watercolor presented detail of the county lot fence as a post and

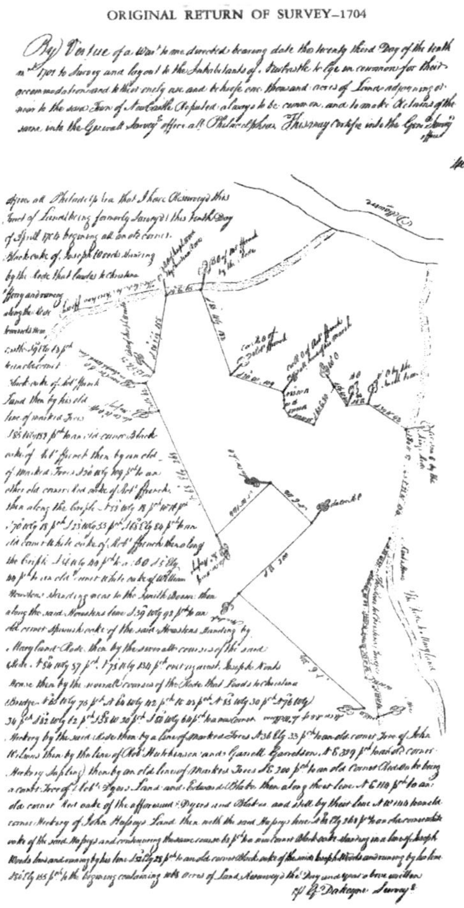

Left: *Original Return of Survey—1704*. In this map of the Common, the Delaware River is at the top right, with the village of New Castle along it, bounded by roads to Christiana Bridge, Maryland and the Christiana Ferry. The first boundary lines represent the end of the village and the beginning of the Common, which stretches to the second boundary lines. *Courtesy Trustees of the Common.*

Below: *Evolution of the Court House, 1732–1845.* The drawing shows how the Courthouse grew from a central block of 1732, adding a portion of the east wing in 1765, but not until 1805 was it full size, while the west wing did not appear in brick until 1845. *Courtesy Timothy Mullin.*

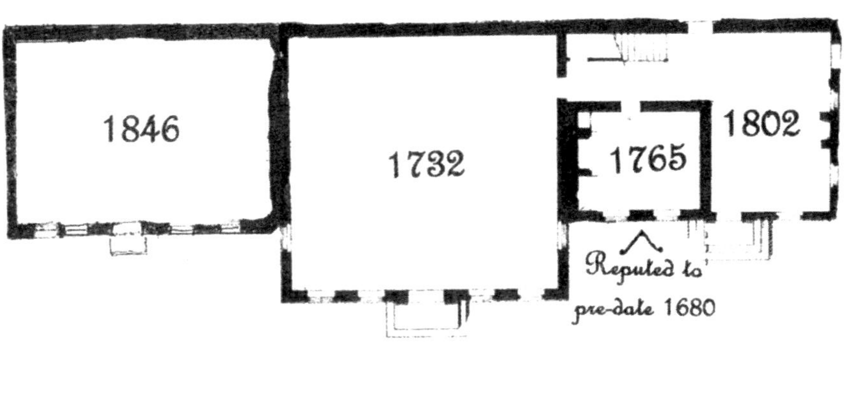

rail structure, covered by four levels of wooden planks. It is noteworthy that three ornamental rather than shade trees line the outside of the fence. They have elaborate wooden protectors at their bases, indicating that animals like pigs might root them up. However, it appears that the fence and plantings are conjectural, a proposal by Latrobe rather than reality. Elsewhere, trees are also in Latrobe's view behind the courthouse, but on the whole the Green is devoid of landscaping. A well-worn path runs from one of the Delaware Street gates to the edge of Immanuel's burial yard. Visible is the burial yard masonry wall, broken by two ornamental pillars that support a wooden gate. While no livestock or people appear in the view, the tree protectors serve as a reminder that trees on the street had to be shielded from wandering livestock. (See illustration.)

Two years later, three Trustees of the Common—James Riddle, George Read Jr. and James Booth—intervened and urged that the Public Square be made "handsome" by enclosing it anew and ornamenting it with trees. The next year, a committee headed by a trustee was set up to obtain post and rail fencing. The committee purchased the materials, but it was not until October 1809 that Jacob Colesbery was employed to erect and paint the post and rail fence.

An 1822 painting of the Green shows it as fenced and gated, with a post and rail fence at three levels, with the top/fourth level covered with planks. A post and rail gate opens along Delaware Street, and a fancier pointed iron gate is in the rear, which serves as the entrance to the Immanuel churchyard. The church burial yard has its own brick wall covered with mortar to make it look smooth. A willow and a few fur trees are on the eastern and western edges of the Green, and Immanuel's burial yard has trees, but they do not create a landscaped space. The Delaware Street front is edged with stone slabs.

Other conditions contributed to ending the use of the Green for pasturing animals. Beginning in 1816 and continuing for several decades, the ownership of livestock by townspeople declined so that in 1828 only a quarter of households kept them. While a few households would maintain cows and pigs in the second half of the nineteenth century, the days of keeping livestock in New Castle were numbered.

Not to be confused with the Green, the Common was land located beyond the town that in English tradition was available to citizens of New Castle for pasture, hay, wood lots, fishing and garden plots—though not settlement. Commons were established in medieval England, Scotland and Ireland chiefly in an effort to attract peasants to manorial lands. They continued to exist traditionally and in English law before William Penn arrived in New Castle in 1682. He planned politically strong townships, whose urban centers drew from the agricultural production of the countryside—a situation that already existed at New Castle. To promote this, Penn granted the town a common that was "for the only use and behoof of the inhabitants of New Castle, to be in common for their accommodation forever." Penn defined it in law from 1701 to 1704 when 1,068 acres were set aside outside the village and surveyed by his order as the proprietor of the Three Lower Counties, which became Delaware. The Common extended around New Castle to the north and west but did not cover the waterfront.

After the colonial wars, New Castle's gentry felt the need for someone to administer the Common. The valuable wood had entirely been cut, and squatters had extended their cultivation into the Common, making a legal entity necessary to remove them. In 1760, twenty-nine gentlemen petitioned the General Assembly of the Three Lower Counties, asking that a body be established to administer the Common. Evidently, the assembly did not respond, so the petitioners passed it on to the proprietor's heirs, Thomas and Richard Penn.

In 1764, the Penns replied affirmatively to the petitioners, appointing Trustees of the Common. They were to annually give the Penns a rent of a single ear of Indian corn, if demanded. Thus, from this date a body of trustees was recognized to act as an executive for the Common. When setting up the trustees, the Penns stipulated that none of the land be sold; instead it had to be kept "for the use of a common for the inhabitants of the town of New Castle." The trustees did not have the right "to grant, bargain, sell, alien,

The Courthouse and the Green, 1805 survey, Benjamin Latrobe, unfinished watercolor. The central part of the Courthouse was built in 1732. Here, on June 15, 1776, the Delaware Assembly unanimously declared Delaware to be separate from the proprietorship of the Penn family and set about establishing a new government. The structure was briefly the capitol of the state of Delaware until 1777. *Courtesy Delaware Public Archives.*

convey, release or confirm" the Common to any person. If the trustees violated these stipulations, the Common would revert to the Penns and their heirs. As a group, the trustees would not be easily caught up in the political controversy over taxes with Britain that was just beginning as they were formed. The New Castle County Committee of thirteen, created a decade later on the Green to support the closing of the port of Boston, had only three trustees on it.

At the center of town, the Courthouse was erected in 1732, the same year construction began on Independence Hall in Philadelphia. The brick structure was in the Georgian style, looking like a large townhouse, its principal decoration being windows in perfect symmetry. Both wings were added later, and while they look similar, the east wing is considerably larger than the other. Its interior was Spartan; costly embellishments would have to come later. In 1750, from the cupola of the courthouse, the famous twelve-mile circle was run as stipulated in William Penn's grant of 1682, which created and still forms the northern boundary of Delaware.

A government meeting building had been erected on the site of the existing courthouse in the 1680s, but we have very little knowledge of it, except that a prisoner, William Kelsey, burned down it and the jail in an attempt to escape in 1729. The new building of 1732 served as the home of the Three Lower Counties Assembly. The privilege had been granted by William Penn in 1704 to the counties of New Castle, Kent and Sussex, which would make up Delaware. The executive remained in the hands of the Penn family, and in practice the governor resided in Philadelphia, although he visited New Castle occasionally. During the colonial period, then, New Castle was the home of an assembly and courts.

The Courthouse's role as a colonial capitol ended symbolically on July 24, 1776, when public presentation of the Declaration of Independence was made in front of it before a crowd and militia, which, after three huzzas, destroyed the symbols of the British monarchy that decorated the building. For the next several months, the Courthouse was capitol of the new state of Delaware and was where the state's first constitution was written and approved. Still, the state government was permanently moved to Dover in 1777. But this did not end the building's political role, as it continued to be the seat of New Castle County until 1882.

As the county seat, a complex developed behind the Courthouse and into the Green. In 1732, along with the new Courthouse, a new jail was erected to replace the one burned by Kelsey. By 1805, the fenced county lot behind the Courthouse included separate structures for a workhouse and jail.

A final civic space is the Town Hall, the only one that did not exist during the Revolutionary era. It was the culmination of the promise of the era, for it offered a place where the business of municipal government could transpire, as well as be a home for its fire companies and the Trustees of the Common. Completed in 1826, meetings held inside allowed these entities to encourage and finance projects in the community aimed at making New Castle an urban center.

Before 1826, the Trustees of the Common and the Town Commissioners met in taverns and private houses, where town meetings were also held. As their purpose only involved New Castle, these entities made no effort to meet in the Courthouse, which was the center of state and county government.

The Town Hall was planned by a committee of the Trustees of the Common from June 1823 to July 1825, when construction actually began. It was completed a little more than a year later in September 1826, fifty years after New Castle had declared its independence from Britain. The Trustees of the Common called for a structure that was three stories, with finished plaster ceilings, a four-way pitched roof, a cupola with small windows—placed in the midst of the roof—thirteen windows, copper flashing and drain pipes at the front corners of the building. It was to have a three-part cupola with surrounding rail, a hipped roof, a rear chimney for fireplaces and two rear three-over-three windows. What you see today is a brick structure, built on a brick floor, that looks square, but it is in fact thirty-eight feet wide by thirty-four feet deep.

During the planning process for the Town Hall in October 1823, the Union Fire Company presented a request to the Trustees of the Common to build an engine house. A room above would serve as a meeting space for the Town Commissioners and the Trustees of the Common. The firemen's plan for a town hall was combined with the trustees' plan. The firemen eventually moved into the first-floor spaces on either side of the central passageway.

By visiting these five civic spaces, you will be able to see how New Castle evolved from a colonial hamlet to a fledgling city. The Market House was an important urban amenity for the town and was meant to protect the quality of the perishable products that the average person consumed. The Green is the oldest civic space in New Castle and was the scene of protest against the tyranny of the British Parliament. The Trustees of the Common took surrounding territory that had been conceived of as a resource to be shared by all of New Castle's inhabitants and, after the Revolution, turned it into a source of revenue for capital projects that improved the town. The Town Hall, erected at the end of the Revolutionary era, was meant by the Trustees of the Common to give the town's local government a boost. The Courthouse performed the role of bringing politics from another place into New Castle while also dispensing justice to the local community. Collectively, the five civic spaces were symbols of New Castle's role as an autonomous community during the Revolutionary era.

New Castle in the Era of Revolution

Defining New Castle in terms of its civic spaces is important because during much of its history, including the Revolution, it was not a municipality. Not until 1797 did it obtain a government from the Delaware Assembly, and even then it was not chartered and the document was purposely restrictive. For local government, William Penn had divided the Three Lower Counties into hundreds, a situation unique to Delaware. New Castle and its immediate area were New Castle Hundred, one of nine hundreds in 1775 that made up New Castle County.

Established in 1682 for the purpose of taxation, the hundred was an English Saxon land division. The hundred also served as a judicial and legislative district. By 1775, the hundreds closest to New Castle were Red Lion and St. George's to the south, Pencader and White Clay Creek to the west and Christiana and Brandywine to the north. Thus, in documentation it is not always clear which New Castle is designated. Our story also carries us beyond these boundaries to all of Delaware, the nearby metropolis of Philadelphia and the broad Delmarva Peninsula, consisting of the Eastern Shore of Maryland and Virginia as well as Delaware.

New Castle's People

The peopling of New Castle was a long process. After the early years of Dutch and Swedish occupation, newcomers from the late seventeenth

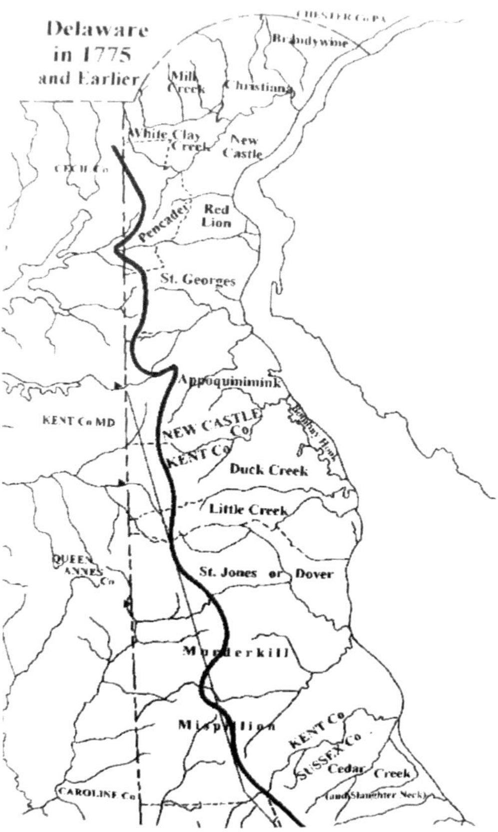

Map with hundreds in 1775. Originally established in 1682 by William Penn for the purposes of taxation, the hundred is an English land division. New Castle had its own hundred, of which the town of New Castle was the center. *Courtesy Delaware Genealogical Society.*

century primarily came from the British Isles and nearby Maryland and Virginia seeking opportunities in New Castle as lawyers, merchants, sailors, servants and farmers.

Some who worked in New Castle were involved in the legislature or law courts when government was present at the Courthouse. As noted, New Castle was the seat of the Lower Counties Assembly, a privilege granted by William Penn and continued by his descendants. Buildings like Cloud's Row were erected in 1801 by Chester County, Pennsylvania builder Harlan Cloud to attract attorneys on court business and provide offices, lodging and homes.

In 1764, William Penn's heirs, Thomas and Richard, appointed thirteen citizens as Trustees of the Common. They represented colonial New Castle's leadership. These original trustees were John Finney, Richard McWilliam, David Finney, Thomas McKean, George Read Sr., Dr. George Munro, John Van Gezell, Zachariah Van Leuvenigh, Slator Clay, John Yeates, Nathaniel Silsbee, Daniel McLonen and Robert Morrison. McKean and Read would be most active in the Revolution, signing the Declaration of Independence. McKean was related to many of them and would serve as a trustee of their loan office. Van Leuvenigh, married to Ann Armitage, was McKean's brother-in-law. McWilliam, like Read, was a justice of the king's court. They were mostly legal minds, sharing a concern for family

Above: Cloud's Row, 1801–1804. Named for Chester County, Pennsylvania builder Harlan Cloud, this row is designed with one room per floor, rising three stories high. Built on speculation, the rooms were popular as attorneys' offices and residences when county court was in session.

Left: *Pepper-pot*, by John Lewis Kimmel, 1811. He was a German immigrant who worked in Philadelphia between 1809 and 1821. The painting shows the interior of a Philadelphia market house, with people of every class congregating there. *Courtesy Philadelphia Museum of Art.*

property that fostered intermarriage and a respect for English law and the British Constitution.

With a population of about five hundred to eight hundred, New Castle became "a rowdy place of seafaring laborers whose ethnic and racial identities reinforced their low social status." We get an idea of who frequented our civic spaces in a portrayal of a market group in a genre painting of John Lewis Kimmel. He emigrated from Germany to Philadelphia and in 1811 painted *Pepper-pot*, depicting a simmering soup at a market that is surrounded by people of diverse social classes. The barefoot free black saleswoman not only made the soup but also provided bowls, spoons and a ladle for the pewter pot. The old man is apparently a Revolutionary War veteran, while the presence of the young girls shows that they were permitted to go to the noisy market. The mother and son are well dressed, representing the elite. An artisan or laborer is portrayed by the tall young man. The pot itself contained a thick soup made from tripe, ox feet and considerable spices—often made so that a "hungry man can get a healthy meal for only a few cents." New Castle's market must have had the same environment, providing food and entertainment for every part of society.

AFRICAN AMERICANS AS SLAVES AND SAILORS

Slavery was a longstanding institution in New Castle and legally existed until the end of the Civil War. In 1664, a cargo of thirty-eight males and thirty-four females is the first record of slaves being imported from Africa into New Castle by the Dutch. It is estimated that slaves already in the Dutch colony made up about one-fifth to one-fourth of the town's population. Slavery continued under English rule and the Penn family's proprietorship of the region that became Delaware. After the early imports, most slaves came to the New Castle area with their masters from Maryland and Virginia, when families like the Reads or Bedfords migrated. A few slaves were sailors, hired out by their masters to work on ships, a situation that was lucrative for both master and slave. By the end of the eighteenth century, a third of the area's population was probably black, although more of them lived in the countryside, where they cultivated the cash crops of tobacco and wheat.

The Rise of Freedmen

In the decade after the Revolution, two out of three blacks in New Castle County were still slaves, showing that the Independence movement had done little to change the situation. In the 1790s, however, the process of freeing slaves in New Castle Hundred flourished so that there were now almost two free blacks for every slave. The growth of free blacks was effected by acts of the state legislature, although it still upheld slavery. It encouraged manumission, voluntary individual acts by masters that freed their slaves. Throughout most of the eighteenth century, the Delaware Assembly had not been sympathetic to manumission, requiring that slave owners post a bond of thirty pounds on newly emancipated freed men who were over thirty years old or infirm, fearing that they would be indigent. Later, the assembly expanded the bond to all persons freed from slavery and raised it to sixty pounds, while all free blacks, not just the aged, were subject to it. This changed from 1787 on, as the assembly dismantled these laws in order to create a more sympathetic atmosphere for manumission.

Certain masters, especially Quakers, were motivated to manumit by enlightened ideas about the equality of mankind. Others found the staple crop system and their inability to sell slaves outside of Delaware unprofitable and made an economic decision that they no longer could afford slaves. From the slaves' standpoint, manumission was not as easy as it sounds because while many masters agreed to free their slaves, they attached conditions, and their heirs tried to ignore such agreements. Manumission also had little connection with the antislavery movement, let alone the abolition of slavery, since those who manumitted their slaves often went on to acquire more, chiefly manumitting slaves who were old and unproductive to replace them with younger slaves.

As a result of the rise in the number of freedmen, an extensive population of mixed-race maritime and agricultural workers developed. New Castle's port was closely tied to that of Philadelphia, where many free blacks were sailors. Freedmen found opportunity in Philadelphia's port on ships or as stevedores, and federal protection certificates from 1796 show that freedmen constituted one-fifth of the port's seamen. The certificates also indicate the birthplaces of the freedmen, and a substantial number were from the Delmarva region, including Delaware, so that New Castle's freedmen were likely to find work at Philadelphia's port as well as their hometown and moved back and forth between the two ports.

What was it like to be a freedman in early nineteenth-century New Castle? Of those who had occupations, most black males were laborers, ages thirteen to ninety-five, and most black females were servants, ages eleven to eighty-five. Men usually headed a household, and some were sailors, coachmen, bricklayers or carpenters. A few were even entrepreneurs who kept oyster houses, livery stables or hairdresser shops. Women did not necessarily have their own households; rather, as servants they lived in white households or establishments like inns, where they worked. Still, black families were an enduring part of New Castle's population.

SCOTS-IRISH SERVANTS

The Scots-Irish originated when Presbyterian Scots immigrated to and settled in Ireland in the seventeenth and eighteenth centuries, encouraged by various schemes of the English monarchy and the Irish aristocracy. Economic restructuring and memories of religious discrimination—which eased after the Glorious Revolution in 1688—led them to migrate farther to North America. But many could not afford the passage, so they indentured themselves as servants. Some came to New Castle, one of the first ports up the Delaware River to be reached after a harrowing transatlantic voyage. In 1729, an extraordinary "2000 Irish people" were reported to have landed in a week at New Castle, although one hundred of them had died in the passage. While the annual numbers declined to more like two hundred to five hundred in the 1730s, Scots-Irish immigration to New Castle continued throughout the eighteenth century as Delaware River merchants sent flaxseed to the Irish linen industry and received servants on the return voyage. While some Scots-Irish stayed in New Castle, most spread elsewhere, especially north to Philadelphia and south to Maryland and Virginia. Although dominant in the emigration, the Scots-Irish were joined by considerable numbers of ethnic groups from other parts of the British Isles, namely Scots, English, Welch, Palatines resettled from the Rhineland and Huguenots resettled from France.

Thus, in the eighteenth century, Scots-Irish servants made up an important segment of New Castle's population. They mixed easily with the remains of Dutch, Swedish and Quaker elements that had settled in the seventeenth century. Indenturing required that once most Scots-Irish arrived they would be legally bound to a master for a period of three to seven years to work off the cost. Having experienced New Castle masters, some servants felt themselves as abused as if they had been slaves. Masters liked the deal and tried to increase the workload and duration of servitude illegally, forcing many servants to disappear just like runaway slaves. When the indenture was completed, William Penn's government awarded the free man one new suit, ten bushels of wheat or fourteen of corn, one axe, two hoes and, at first, fifty acres of land. So it was worth it.

Those Scots-Irish servants who stayed in New Castle rose in numbers and built the Presbyterian meetinghouse in 1707 as a sign of their influence. Fifteen years later, George Ross, the Anglican pastor at Immanuel Church, was envious of their growth, calling them "the bitterest railers against [his] Church that ever trod upon American ground." Two of Delaware's signers of the Declaration of Independence, Thomas McKean and George Read, were from families who had emigrated from Ireland. Not all Irish Protestants were Presbyterians, however, for Read's family was from the Pale around Dublin, where Anglicanism prevailed.

Farmers

Farmers were the third part of the citizen mix, though they were divided between the planters, or wealthy plantation owners, and the vast majority, who were small holders and even poor. While most cultivated land in the surrounding hundreds, they traded and went to church in New Castle and were an integral part of New Castle's economic and social life. In the 1780s, unlike Sussex and Kent Counties, where the vast majority were subsistence small holders, a majority of those in New Castle County were commercial farmers of some scale, selling their produce outside their community, exporting wheat, which had replaced tobacco in the 1730s as the dominant staple. The two richest commercial agricultural areas in the state were south of New Castle, Red Lion and St. George's Hundreds and were tied to New Castle's port and market. New Castle and Dover Hundreds shared honors as the wealthiest communities in the state with the greatest number of large property owners, many of whom were planters.

New Castle's elite of merchants or lawyers also needed farms to support their homes in town. The farms became seasonal retreats, especially in autumn, when the fever and ague prevailed in town. These farms furnished fuel and necessities beyond what was in the kitchen garden or at the market so that the elite did not have to use the market. George Read Sr.'s home on Front Street (the Strand) had supporting farms, the first of which was Stonum, developed from 1763 to 1769, while the substantial brick country house you see today dates from a decade later. Read also had two lots near New Castle, perhaps within the Common, for hay and pasturing his horses

Stonum, one of George Read Sr.'s country houses, circa 1780. He needed supporting farms for his home on Front Street, the first of which was Stonum, developed from 1763 to 1769. These farms furnished fuel and necessities beyond what was in the kitchen garden so that the elite did not have to use the market. Investment in productive land made one a gentleman.

and cows. However, to build substantial country estates, one had to go beyond the Common.

After the Revolution, farmers who made a living by selling wheat or flaxseed surplus received a boost when the Trustees of the Common became able to rent the Common. The development of the market also helped farmers because they became its chief suppliers when they came to New Castle's Market House and shambles two days a week. Still, agricultural production declined in the nineteenth century as estates were split into smaller parcels and farmland lost its value, while many free blacks moved to the countryside to work on farms, where the cost of living was cheaper than in New Castle. In the early 1800s, New Castle Hundred became more like the conditions in Kent and Sussex Counties.

English Institutions

English institutions were important to the organization of New Castle and its hundred, in the creation of the five civic spaces and in the protest against the effort of the English Parliament to tax its colonies. The community was dominated by numerous immigrants from the British Isles. An English communal spirit, not individual capitalistic inspiration, created the Market House, the Green, the Common, the Courthouse and the Town Hall. The Common, of medieval English origin, was unique to New Castle. With so many lawyers practicing at the Courthouse, the points of English common law were unusually respected. Market houses and town halls abounded in England to serve as models for those in New Castle. The community could not be neutral when the actions of Parliament appeared threatening.

John Dickinson's Letters

The appreciation of English institutions and traditions was alive and well in the mid-1760s when the colonists protested the Stamp Act and Townshend Duties on paper, glass, paint and, most famously, tea. John Dickinson of Pennsylvania and Delaware, a Quaker attorney and gentleman farmer, wrote twelve letters that were an immediate sensation in the press on both sides of the Atlantic, selling more copies in pamphlet form than any publication before. Educated at home in Delaware, owner of a country plantation in Kent County and eventually president of Delaware, Dickinson was a friend to many of New Castle's political leaders, including George Read, Thomas McKean and James Booth, whose convictions were influenced by Dickinson. In the letters, he claimed to live near the banks of the Delaware River, on a small farm where "my servants are few, and good: I have a little money at interest; I wish for no more…I am completing the number of days allotted to me by divine goodness." He directed his letters to solid middle-class farmers, although he admitted to spending a good deal of time in his library, a luxury not available to most farmers, of whom a substantial minority were illiterate.

Dickinson needed his extensive library because he wrote his letters in the Whig tradition, based on English history and experience rather than the right reason of the Enlightenment. He used the English constitutional history found in his books to support his arguments. For example, the Glorious Revolution of 1688 provided him with information on the much-admired ascent to the English throne of William and Mary, ending the reign of the supposedly

Mezzotint of John Dickinson by John Forest after Charles Willson Peale, 1782–83. A resident of Pennsylvania and Delaware, Dickinson was a Quaker attorney and gentleman farmer who wrote *Letters From a Farmer in Pennsylvania*, an immediate sensation on both sides of the Atlantic, supporting colonial protest against the policies of Parliament. *Courtesy Library of Congress, Prints and Photographs.*

misguided Stuarts. The couple had been chosen by Parliament, giving that body the right to determine the monarchy's succession, and just as crucial, William was a Calvinist, a king who would ease the burdens of dissenting Protestants. On the basis of history, Dickinson offered a peaceful but firm means of opposing Parliament's efforts to tax the colonies.

In letter three, Dickinson argued that while the people in the colonies were in danger, the cause of liberty had "too much dignity to be sullied by turbulence and tumult" brought on by riots. Disrespecting the Crown and mother country would "injure the reputation of the people as to wisdom, valor, and virtue, without procuring them the least benefit." Petition by assemblies to the Parliament and Crown should be the principal means of protest. Hostile to any thought of independence or violence, Dickinson asserted that "the prosperity of these provinces is founded in their dependence on Great Britain."

In the fourth letter, Dickinson took on the distinction that had been made between the Stamp Act as an internal tax and the Townshend Duties as external taxes because they were duties on items of trade like tea. He would have none of this idea. In the constitution and history of England, a tax was "an imposition on the subject, for the sole purpose of levying money"; thus, no distinction between internal and external existed. He went on to quote the American "bill of rights" that had been formulated at the Stamp Act Congress in 1765. Article 3 stated that it was the undoubted right of Englishmen that no tax be imposed on them except with their own consent.

Articles 4 and 5 concurred that the colonists could not be represented in the House of Commons and that the only taxes that could be levied on them would be done by their own legislatures. He also discussed the relationship of the colonies within the British Empire, noting that it was administered "to [the colonies'] mutual advantage." Again, while the colonies should oppose the efforts of Parliament to levy taxes, they should point out their record of peaceful submission as a means of impressing English authorities. Empire and liberty were compatible.

Dickinson put his faith in the protest and the ability of colonial assemblies to check the power of governors. The assemblies were to provide for defense, administer justice through courts and support civil government. On defense, he was concerned that even if funds were needed for important fortifications, the levying of such money still required an assembly's consent. On the courts, as a practicing attorney, Dickinson found them wanting, especially as the judiciary was more artful than high-minded and was not independent from the assemblies. As to civil government, Dickinson compared assemblymen to "Roman Senators" but feared that once an assembly had granted the requests of the Crown, they would fall into disuse, no longer playing an important role in the English Constitution. With all their imperfections, the assemblies were still the best hope of ensuring the liberty and happiness of their constituents.

Overall, Dickinson recognized the abuse of the Crown's ministers and Parliament, which had to be vigorously protested. Yet this was to be done prudently, within the framework of the British Constitution and the ability of the colonies to maintain a place in the British Empire. As long as Dickinson's views were held, no possibility of justifying independence existed. He concluded that "if the unresolved sense of these colonies is immediately expressed by resolves of assemblies…and by petitions to the crown and parliament for redress, these measures, will have the same success now that they had in the time of the Stamp Act." Here was a blueprint for protest against the arbitrary power of Parliament that would be in effect for almost a decade, but it would lead the colonies into civil war with the mother country, a consequence that Dickinson abhorred. By sticking to his principles, Dickinson's influence would remain important until 1774, but after that, he would lose friends and support as independence became the watchword.

Churches in the Independence Movement

While they were not exactly civic spaces because of their denominational requirements, churches were meeting spaces, and congregations provided leadership that would give them roles in the Independence movement. While earlier New Castle had hosted Dutch Reformed and Lutheran congregations and then a Quaker meeting, the Revolutionary era was dominated by only two: New Castle Presbyterian Church and Immanuel Anglican Church. Their ascendancy in a community known for its religious toleration dated from about 1700, when houses of worship were erected by both denominations, as well as a Quaker meetinghouse. It is argued the New Castle's gentry supported the construction of these structures as sign that New Castle was no longer a mere trading post but rather a genuine town.

New Castle's Presbyterian Meetinghouse

New Castle's Presbyterian meetinghouse was built in 1707 on two lots purchased for twenty-two pounds from Thomas Janvier and John Brewster. Janvier was a Huguenot who had settled in New Castle about 1685, was naturalized ten years later and obtained considerable property on Front Street in the following years. In 1709, he was a ruling elder of the Presbyterian Church. A structure was needed because Reverend John Wilson was holding Presbyterian services in the government house, and the Anglicans and Quakers had their own buildings underway. A three-bay

The New Castle Presbyterian meetinghouse, 1930s. The meetinghouse was erected in 1707 and expanded in the mid-eighteenth century. Growing numbers of Presbyterian indentured servants from Ireland and Scotland made it their church. Pastor Joseph Montgomery and the congregation became the center of New Castle's Independence movement. *Courtesy Don Reese.*

brick structure was erected in 1707, about half the size of the building you see today. By the time of the Revolution, the meetinghouse had doubled in size to the present proportions, reflecting the growth of its congregation. For the Scots-Irish and other dissenting migrants, the Presbyterian Church was their first choice.

PRESBYTERIANS BEYOND NEW CASTLE

In 1717, the newly organized New Castle Presbytery included congregations at New Castle, Head of Christiana, Appoquinimy (Drawyers) and the Welsh Tract. Over the next sixty years, effort was made to place Presbyterian meetinghouses in the leading settlement of each hundred, so that at the beginning of the Revolution, there were more Presbyterian congregations in

New Castle County than any other denomination. One of the strengths of New Castle's meetinghouse was that it was the center of these Presbyterian congregations. Active congregations came to exist throughout New Castle County in Brandywine Hundred (Wilmington), Appoquinimy Hundred (Drawyers), Christiana Hundred (centered at the head navigation or bridge on the Christina River), St. George's Hundred, Pencader Hundred (Welsh Tract), White Clay Creek Hundred (Newark) and Red Clay Creek.

However, the number of congregations should not be taken as a sign of great strength, for many were fledgling and had no meetinghouse or settled minister. Some were too small to afford such luxuries, and at first most were run by elders with the exception of an occasional visit from a traveling minister sent by the Presbytery. One solution was to have two or more congregations come together to support a single minister. New Castle's Reverend John Wilson had first preached on alternative weeks at Christiana Bridge in 1706, and New Castle's ministers continued to serve that congregation when its congregation was willing. Elsewhere at the time of the Revolution, Reverend William McKennan served both Red Clay Creek and White Clay Creek. However, these cooperative relationships lasted only for the duration of a minister's tenure.

Portrait of James Latimer, by Clawsin S. Hammitt after Charles Willson Peale, circa 1914. A Scots-Irishman, Latimer lived in Christiana Hundred at Newport and attended the Christiana Presbyterian meetinghouse. He became a lieutenant colonel of the New Castle County militia and a member of the New Castle County Council of Safety. *Original maintained by the Senate Commission on Art, Washington, D.C.*

These congregations sustained New Castle County's leadership in the independence movement. For instance, Scots-Irish leaders like James Latimer of nearby Newport attended the Christiana Presbyterian meetinghouse. Born in Ulster in 1736, as a youth Latimer migrated with his family to Chester, Pennsylvania, and after he married in 1749, he moved to Newport on the Christiana River. He had entered the shipping business from Philadelphia, sailing twice a year to Ulster.

In Christiana, he operated flour mills and shipped grain and produce to Philadelphia and the West Indies. With military experience in the Seven Years' War, Latimer became a lieutenant colonel of the New Castle County militia in the Revolutionary War. In 1775, he was named a member of the New Castle County Council of Safety. In the winter of 1776–77, he helped supply Washington's army encamped on the Delaware River. Latimer was also elected a New Castle County justice of the court of common pleas and the orphan's court. He was typical of the combination of political, economic and military talent found in Presbyterian meetinghouses.

PRESBYTERIANS DEBATE THE POSSIBILITY OF INDEPENDENCE

The question of the influence of religion on the Independence movement has often been ignored because it is complicated. One source of inspiration for independence is based on the history of dissent in the British Isles. The dissenting tradition depended on Calvinist organization, examples from the Bible and the literature of Protestant martyrs. Dissenters were those Protestant denominations that did not accept the umbrella of the Anglican Church, preferring from the time of the Elizabethan Compromise to go their own way. Often they were hostile to the "popish" liturgy of the Anglican Church, which they felt still clung to its Roman Catholic roots. The Crown favored the Anglican establishment because it offered a means of political unity, and Parliament reacted by restricting the dissenting chapels and limiting their political rights—though the dissenters were tolerated as a group. Fluctuations in their treatment, especially of their leaders, led some dissenters to immigrate to America, where they hoped to set up godly communities without restrictions. In much of New England, they were able to do this by establishing themselves as the state-supported Congregational Church, exercising similar authority as the Anglican Church did in the British Isles.

Like the Congregational Church, the Church of Scotland was established and tax-supported, although a Presbyterian church. During the seventeenth century, when the Stuarts were monarchs of both England and Scotland, the Church of Scotland gradually lost its favored position as the Stuarts introduced Anglican practices into the liturgy. This upset some Scots and encouraged them to rebel and migrate. However, the Glorious Revolution of William and Mary in 1690 restored the established position to the Church of

Scotland. This event would be remembered, as Dickinson's letters showed, as a time when Presbyterians and dissenters were freed of many restrictions in the practice of their faith. The history of dissent, then, described times when the Crown and Parliament had enacted legislation that dissenters had vigorously protested, so that when the colonies protested, the dissenters were already experienced.

Another source of ideas for the independence movement was the philosophy of the Enlightenment. These ideas had infiltrated the British Isles from the Continent, chiefly because enlightened thinkers found Britain to be the perfect example of an enlightened state. Right reason and the laws of nature were the first principles of the Enlightenment. Most of the Founding Fathers at Philadelphia in 1776 were deists who accepted the authority of right reason based on the ideals of the Enlightenment. Deists did not believe in the divinity of Christ, so it would be wrong to call them Christians. Nevertheless, deism was never an organized religion; rather, it was a philosophical tradition that believed in a rational God and was adaptable to traditional religion. To deists, piety was a civic virtue. Thus, a religious element existed in the Enlightenment, for many of the Founding Fathers attended religious services and saw the need to cultivate religion to stabilize society.

The tradition of dissent and the Enlightenment came together in Scotland, where the Universities of Edinburgh and Glasgow were leading centers of natural law and educated the ministers of the Church of Scotland and Ulster. When Scottish or Scots-Irish divines reached American soil, they were already familiar with the Enlightenment, as well as the history of Presbyterian dissent.

Reverends Francis Alison and John Witherspoon

Francis Alison disembarked at New Castle in 1735. He was a Scots-Irishman who had been exposed to the Enlightenment at the University of Glasgow. Two years later, he was ordained a minister by the New Castle Presbytery and sent to the New London congregation in southeastern Pennsylvania. Alison also sought to establish a school at his home, and six years later, it commenced with the support of the presbyteries of New Castle, Philadelphia and Donegal, Alison's home Presbytery in Ulster. He was antagonistic toward George Whitefield's outdoor gatherings that spread through the region in

1739. Instead, he taught Old Side Presbyterianism to pupils like Thomas McKean and George Read, who would become New Castle's leaders in the Revolution. Young McKean boarded with the Alison family for nine years and in the school was exposed to Latin, Greek, mathematics, rhetoric, logic and moral philosophy. Alison's curriculum was based on Professor Francis Hutcheson's enlightened ideas, for even though in Pennsylvania, Alison corresponded with him at the University of Glasgow. Thus Alison, through Hutcheson, was the first to offer systematic instruction to his pupils in the philosophy of the Scottish Enlightenment.

Alison was further involved with New Castle and McKean because he married Hannah Armitage, whose father, James Armitage, was a justice of the New Castle Court of Common Pleas. Her sister, Sally Armitage, would become McKean's second wife. Although Alison left New London to teach at the College of Philadelphia (later the University of Pennsylvania), he remained as trustee of the school, which in 1767 was moved to Newark, Delaware, where it was not interrupted until the British invasion ten years later. In the 1760s, Alison led Presbyterian opposition to the Stamp Act and Townshend

The Revd Mr. Alison, circa 1750. His teachings and views were influenced by the Scottish Enlightenment and Old School Presbyterianism. His school, the New London Academy in southeastern Pennsylvania, was regarded as one of the best in the region, and it attracted pupils like New Castle's Thomas McKean and George Read. *Courtesy of the Presbyterian Minister's Fund, Historical Society of Pennsylvania.*

Duties. He was also wary of efforts by Anglican leaders in the colonies to establish a bishop or, for that matter, any established church. Once the war began, he supported it, but ultimately he felt that he was too much of a scholar to become directly involved in the conflict; he died in 1779.

Another immigrant from the British Isles, arriving in Philadelphia in 1768, was John Witherspoon, a Presbyterian minister from the synod of Glasgow and Ayr. As a Scot, he was in a minority when compared with the numerous Scots-Irish. No ordinary Presbyterian minister, he involved himself in politics and would be a delegate to Congress, where he would be appointed Congressional chaplain by President John Hancock. He would be the only clergyman to sign the Declaration of Independence.

Born at Gifford, East Lothian, Scotland, Witherspoon obtained a Master of Arts from the University of Edinburgh in 1739, where he was exposed to the Scottish Enlightenment. He became a Church of Scotland minister and was also awarded a doctorate of divinity from the University of St. Andrews. At the persistent urging of Dr. Benjamin Rush of Philadelphia, Witherspoon finally agreed to become president and head professor of the Presbyterian College of New Jersey. He was the sixth president of the college, later known as Princeton University. As the college's primary occupation at the time was training ministers, Witherspoon was an influential Presbyterian voice as he traveled to raise money and recruit students for the college.

Witherspoon had an approach to morality that was more influenced by the Scottish philosophers Francis Hutcheson and Thomas Reid than Presbyterian theology. He believed that morality was a science. It could be cultivated in his students or deduced through the development of the moral sense—an ethical compass instilled by God in all human beings and developed through education or sociability. Such an approach to morality was derived from the natural laws of the Enlightenment rather than sources of Christian ethics. While public religion was an important source of social virtue, it was not the only source. Witherspoon, in accordance with the Scottish moral sense philosophy, taught that all human beings could be virtuous. He brought this form of Presbyterianism to New Jersey.

Witherspoon followed his political instincts and joined New Jersey's Somerset County Committee of Correspondence and Safety in early 1774. While he was personally gravitating toward independence, when he went to the Presbyterian Synod of May 1775, he pulled his punches for the sake of synod unity, maintaining a respect for both the king and the Continental Congress. Exactly one year later, Congress called one of its many days of fasting and public prayer, at which Witherspoon presented a sermon, "The

Portrait of John Witherspoon, by Rembrandt Peale, after Charles Willson Peale, 1794. When Witherspoon arrived in Philadelphia in 1768, he was a Presbyterian minister, widely respected in Scotland. While other Presbyterian ministers hesitated, he became involved in politics and would be a delegate to the Continental Congress and the only clergyman to sign the Declaration of Independence. *Courtesy National Portrait Gallery, Smithsonian Institution; partial gift of Mrs. Samuel Mathews.*

Dominion of Providence over the Passions of Men." He particularly aimed the sermon at Scots who were lagging in support for Congress. His sermon would be published in many editions, and it gained him election as a New Jersey delegate to the Continental Congress. There, during the debate over independence, when it was objected that the country was not yet ready for it, according to tradition, he replied that it "was not only ripe for the measure, but in danger of rotting for the want of it." In Congress, Witherspoon would work directly with Delaware leaders like John Dickinson, Thomas McKean and George Read.

THE PRESBYTERIAN SYNOD

Witherspoon was a member of the New York and Philadelphia Presbyterian Synod, where in 1775 his views were still regarded as radical when he went to a poorly attended synod meeting in New York. A committee drafted the synod's pastoral letter reflecting the public attitude of most Presbyterian leaders just after the bloodshed at Lexington and Concord but before the

Declaration of Independence. The pastoral letter described King George III as one "who has merited well of his subjects on many accounts, and who has probably been misled into the late and present measures by those about him." The leaders disavowed any "desire of separation from the parent state…and reconciliation…is [our] most ardent desire." At the same time, they supported the new Continental Congress then sitting in Philadelphia, urging that it "be treated with respect and encouraged in their difficult service." Thus at this time, Congress and the king—but not the Parliament—were compatible.

The chief reason the synod compromised was that the ministers feared civil war. The synod called for "a regard to order and the public peace… so that the evils inseparable from civil war may not be augmented by wantonness and irregularity." As with Dickinson, their protest was not to involve the mob or violence against property. Instead, they pleaded for humanity and mercy to offset the terrible dangers of civil war. For "civil wars are carried on with a rancor and spirit of revenge much greater than those between independent states. The injuries received or supposed in civil wars wound more deeply than those of foreign enemies." To prevent civil war, they recommended meekness and gentleness of spirit. The synod did call for frequent public and private sessions of prayer, as well as gentleness of spirit. It closed with the members' own prayer "that the present unnatural dispute may be speedily terminated by an equitable and lasting settlement on constitutional principles." Clearly the letter was not a call for independence, which, it warned, would cause a violent civil war. With Witherspoon, however, this warning would not be enough to counteract his support of the Independence movement.

New Castle's Presbyterian Meetinghouse

Sentiment for independence in New Castle's Presbyterian meetinghouse was more definite than at the Presbyterian Synod. In 1776, in sizing up the support for independence, John Dickinson was warned that "Colonel [Thomas] McKean is a true Presbyterian and joins the violents…He is suspected of Independency." Similarly, Delaware historian John Monroe wrote of politics in the years before the Revolutionary War that "through these years a notable development in the assembly was the emergence of a Presbyterian party. Thomas McKean, John Haslet and such allies as William Killen [future chancellor of Delaware] and John McKinly [first president of Delaware under the new constitution of 1776] were frequently found voting together in a minority." Monroe felt that they represented an emerging force, "the voice of the new immigrant element in the Delaware counties, especially New Castle and Kent, but their importance lay in 1775 when they gained allies among the older elements in pressing a vigorous anti-English policy."

Monroe pointed out the crucial role of Presbyterians like Thomas McKean in the emerging independence movement. McKean was born in 1734 into a Scots-Irish tavern keeper's family in Chester, Pennsylvania. As noted, he attended Francis Alison's Presbyterian Academy in New London. At the age of sixteen, he moved to New Castle to study law in the library of his wealthy cousin, David Finney. In 1765, at the Stamp Act Congress, his hostility to the British Constitution appeared, and it never diminished. From his arrival, he was a member of the New Castle Presbyterian Church, which would prove to be a center of independence and republicanism. He left New Castle in 1774, drawn to Philadelphia, although he kept a house in New Castle, representing Delaware in the Continental Congress. It was this Congress that commanded his loyalty and allowed him to promote the Declaration of Independence, although he did not sign it until January 1777. In his later life as a lawyer and politician, he was attracted by the opportunities in Pennsylvania, where he served as chief justice and governor. Not always a diplomat, his opinions created many enemies, but he was a consistent supporter of republican government.

Thomas McKean, by Charles Willson Peale, after 1787. From a Scots-Irish family, at the age of sixteen, McKean moved to New Castle to study law in the library of his wealthy cousin, David Finney. From his arrival, he was a member of New Castle Presbyterian Church. In 1765, at the Stamp Act Congress, his hostility to the British Constitution appeared and it never diminished. *Courtesy Wikimedia Commons.*

Thomas McKean, David Finney and John Thompson worshiped in the meetinghouse by the market where Reverend Joseph Montgomery was pastor. All of them were related. Wealthy lawyer David Finney was McKean's mentor and cousin, while his father, Dr. John Finney, was McKean's uncle. McKean would help David Finney to legally obtain his ample inheritance when his father died in 1774. How much law Finney practiced is a matter of debate, for he had no need of an income, but in 1778, he was named a justice of Delaware's Supreme Court. Earlier in the Seven Years' War, both he and McKean had been members of Captain Richard McWilliam's company of militia. Montgomery was a relation of Sally Armitage, McKean's second wife, and he performed their marriage at the meetinghouse in 1774. Montgomery also had a connection with Dr. Benjamin Rush, a Founding Father, through his marriage to Rush's sister, Rachel.

Memorial stones of Thompson family, in New Castle Presbyterian Church yard, 1776, 1790 and 1795. The Thompson family was related to Thomas McKean and supported the Independence movement in New Castle, although they resided on a plantation ten miles to the south. After the war, John became, as the stone says, "Second Justice of the Court of Common Pleas for the County of New Castle."

Dorthe McKean, Thomas's sister, added another name to the McKean network when she married John Thompson, who became McKean's right hand in politics, both representing New Castle County in August 1776 at the convention that wrote the Delaware constitution and in the first assembly elected under the constitution. Of Scots-Irish descent, Thompson was a member of a committee appointed by the assembly in 1777 to investigate the extent of loyalism in Sussex County, which reported in May "a criminal intercourse has been carried on with British Ships of war," both in terms of intelligence and supplies.

Thompson would become, as his memorial in the Presbyterian meetinghouse yard notes, "Second Justice of the Court of Common Pleas for the County of New Castle." He also served for nine years as sheriff of New Castle County. He was competent in arithmetic, surveying and bookkeeping skills. He left New Castle, becoming a planter with farms to the south in New Castle and Red Lion Hundreds, the latter on a creek that flowed into the Delaware River. Here he farmed on a plantation scale with many slaves, his annual wheat crop reaching a value of $1,000 to $1,500. This plantation was the location of the private burial yard from which in the early twentieth century his family remains were removed to the meetinghouse yard.

NEW CASTLE ACCEPTS INDEPENDENCE

In July 1775, on New Castle's Green, another day of fasting was sponsored by the Continental Congress, following its ideal of holding mass meetings to test the faith of the people—as had been done previously by religious leaders in calling for revival meetings. This day of fasting may have been religiously inspired, but it was also a strategy to discover the depth of Congress's support throughout the colonies. The militia formed the core of this gathering, a sign of military support for Congress and also a calming factor for those who feared that the crowd would become rowdy. Churches would vary in support of the fast—some, especially Anglican churches, locking their doors, while other ministers opened them but emphasized conciliation with the king, not independence.

It was a serious crime to avoid participating in Congress's days of fasting. After this day of fasting, the New Castle County Committee of Inspection charged Captain Alexander Porter of the militia with failure to appear and working on that day, as if he were a possible loyalist. He was forced to apologize and state that in the future he would obey the regulations of Congress. His sin that day was to use his slaves to harvest his wheat because he thought it would spoil and because he worried about rumors of a slave rebellion. While his personal reasons were quite plausible, the committee was unmoved because it wanted to make an example of Porter.

In contrast to the evaders, on that day Reverend Joseph Montgomery, the spiritual leader of New Castle's Presbyterian Church, preached a sermon to the militia and community in favor of a war for independence. It came three months after bloodshed at Lexington and Concord but when

Zachariah Van Leuvenigh House, circa 1750. In 1765, Van Leuvenigh purchased this early Georgian-style house with a gambrel and hipped roof at the very edge of the river. During the Revolution, he was chief magistrate of New Castle but refused to accept payment for debt in Continental currency because it was so worthless.

reconciliation was still more popular, as the Presbyterian Synod's May meeting had showed. He was bold in supporting a war for independence, telling the militia to "enlist under the Lord God of Hosts." Montgomery admitted that there was a time when "[w]e loved Great Britain and glowed in her prosperity [and] we boasted in the name of Englishmen." But now he asked for war because the "connection with the parent state must be dissolved." He criticized the Quakers and the Penn family proprietors in both Delaware and Pennsylvania, calling their passive obedience and nonresistance "absurd doctrines." Family ties were included, as the militia would have to fight for their wives, maidens and children, "who look to you for protection." Finally, they were to take God for their "Captain General, and go forth in his strength, keeping the words of his covenant, and doing them, so shall ye prosper in all you do." Calling for war and offering God's leadership was radical at this early stage, when even many of the Founding Fathers like George Read, John Dickinson or John Witherspoon were still defending reconciliation.

Born in Ireland in 1733, Montgomery had come to the region and, at the age of twenty-two, studied at the College of New Jersey; then he went to Newark's Academy. He opened a grammar school in 1757 that educated young men for the ministry. He was licensed as a Presbyterian minister three years later and served congregations in Lewes and Georgetown, Maryland, until he came in 1768 to New Castle, where his charge also included the Christiana congregation. He lived on a farm on the outskirts of New Castle, where his second wife, Rachel Rush Montgomery, was in charge. He would remain unswerving in his support for independence. Three months after his bold speech, he would baptize the son of another member of McKean's extended family, Zachariah Van Leuvenigh, formally naming the infant George Washington, for the new commander in chief of the Continental army. By January 1776, Montgomery would be named chaplain to John Haslet's Delaware Continentals, and after some preparation, he left New Castle to serve with the regiment.

THE WAR'S EFFECT

Some historians have expounded a theory that Baptists, Methodists and New Light Presbyterians provided leadership for the Independence movement because they themselves had already rebelled against their traditional parent organizations, like the Anglican Church and, in the case of Presbyterians, the Old Lights. The ideal that bound these three denominations together is said to have been the religious evangelism that led to open-air revivals and development of congregations that looked to colonial institutions rather than the mother country for authority. As New Castle lacked active Baptist and Methodist churches, it must be asked how this theory played out in its Presbyterian meetinghouse.

The origin of the New Light schism was from 1739, when George Whitefield preached to thousands in New Castle and its county. The upshot of such revivals was the split between New and Old Lights, with the former supporting the need to show piety in an enthusiastic way and the latter emphasizing traditional Calvinist theology—not conduct—in which God predestined salvation. Whitefield left New Castle's congregation divided over these two perspectives, making it difficult to secure a pastor to please all. Nearby, this split had led the New Lights to found the College of New Jersey to educate their ministers, distaining the supply of Old Light ministers that came from Scotland and Ulster and that did find support at the College of Philadelphia.

However, the New Light theory does not ring true for New Castle's meetinghouse. The split was artificial in that open-air religious revivals were as much a way of life with ministers brought up in Scotland and Ulster as in the colonies. What is also overlooked is that Presbyterians realized that the split weakened their meetinghouses, and thus a compromise of coexistence between the two groups was worked out by 1758. With a compromise among Presbyterians, it is difficult to see this religious discord or college rivalry contributing to political controversy over the Stamp Act and Intolerable Acts. True, Reverend Montgomery's preaching outdoors to the militia, urging them to fight, was in the New Light tradition. But beyond this single sermon, we have evidence that he was a theological Old Light in his convictions. In the postwar era, Old Lights would be alive and well in New Castle's meetinghouse.

The meetinghouse congregation failed to sustain its leadership after independence was accepted on July 4, 1776. The loss of Montgomery to the congregation was more of a blow than was realized, for it could find no permanent replacement until 1791. Other Presbyterian ministers were leaving their congregations for the glamour of serving in the rebel army. James Armstrong, probationer of the New Castle Presbytery, became chaplain of Major General John Sullivan's division, while Reverend Elihu Spencer of St. George's Hundred and Reverend John McCreary at Head of Christiana saw some military service.

Those who became chaplains like Montgomery and Armstrong would find that "the camp…was a school of immorality, profanity and vice." Civil order declined and the Sabbath was ignored. Meetinghouses were closed, and the number of representatives sent to the synod meetings declined rapidly. During the war, the preparation of young men for the ministry came to a standstill, even at the College of New Jersey. Thus from 1778 on, the Presbyterian meetinghouse suffered, a sign that the Revolutionary War would be a time of moral and organizational difficulty, fostered by a dreaded civil war.

Moreover, as early as 1773, the New Castle Presbytery had failed to meet, the first of many failures, because "the trouble…war and distress which took place in both the church and the state [had] deranged all affairs, civil and religious for many years and the enemy marching through the Presbytery's bounds occasioned the loss of their old records and…turned fugitive with the enemy." Four years later, the Presbytery's minutes would note that General William Howe's invasion had broken the congregations at New Castle and Christiana Bridge. The war was hard on the Presbyterian meetinghouse.

In the coming of the Revolutionary War in New Castle, Scots-Irish Presbyterians found it easier to favor independence from Great Britain. Combining the traditions of dissent and the Enlightenment, they would lead the cause of independence from Britain, especially in protest gatherings on the Green. In contrast, the Anglicans at Immanuel Church avoided termination of the king of England as the head of their church, becoming a mixture of loyalists and conservative rebels.

Anglican Compromise

Across the Green, when Immanuel Anglican Church was completed in 1708, Presbyterians had actually contributed to the building fund. Yet rivalry appeared between the Presbyterian and Anglican churches in the years before the Independence movement. First it was over a lot on the edge of the Green on which the Anglicans built their sanctuary, claiming it without purchase because it was the king's land and he was the head of their church. Another conflict concerned a bell that had once belonged to the Dutch Reformed Church but had been given to the English blockhouse and then passed to Immanuel. Another concerned George Whitefield, the controversial English evangelist, who preached in New Castle in 1739 on the Green to 2,500 people. Reverend George Ross of Immanuel charged

Immanuel Anglican Church, detail from 1805 survey, Benjamin Latrobe and assistants. It was erected in this form from 1703 to 1708. After the Revolutionary War, it became an Episcopal church. *Courtesy New Castle Historical Society.*

Whitefield with "recommending a set of men among the Presbyterians as unruly as himself, as the only ministers fit to be heard."

Anglicans had started meeting together in New Castle's homes in 1689 and hoped to be inspired by traveling pastors. From 1703 on, effort was made by some of the town's leading citizens to raise funds for a church building. The walls of the structure rose slowly. While it lacked an organ, a royal coat of arms decorated the wall and the gleaming communion set from Queen Anne signified the church's close relationship with the Crown.

Immanuel's leaders sought a missionary from the Society for the Propagation of the Gospel, claiming that "the Presbyterians were gaining ground…by reason of their having a preacher to promote their interest." This English missionary society would become the financial mainstay of the church and was able to send a new rector to Immanuel, George Ross, a former Royal Navy chaplain. Ross would serve the church for five decades, watching the Presbyterians, although he admitted in 1750 that "the church under my care…makes a much meaner appearance than at anytime heretofore." In the eighteenth century, neither this church nor the Presbyterian one would be financially secure.

As protest developed in the 1760s over the right of Parliament to tax the colonies, Anglican churches in the middle colonies were in a quandary. They received favor from the Crown and the Society for the Propagation of the Gospel, so they reciprocated by offering prayers for the monarch. However, Anglican churches were not established or tax-supported, as they were in

Maryland and Virginia. This actually meant that Immanuel Church had much in common with dissenting churches like the Presbyterians, although historically in the British Isles the Anglican Church had opposed dissenters. As the war came, most of Delaware's Anglican churches offered prayers for the king and saw him as reconciling the dispute with the growing Independence movement. But when independence was declared in 1776, most of their priests were forced to discontinue services and close their doors rather than end prayers for the monarch. As an example, Reverend Sydenhame Throne of Milford Parish was brought before the Kent County Committee of Correspondence four times for offering prayers for the king and failing to observe the fasting and prayer days that Congress had promoted. In contrast, New Castle's Immanuel singularly remained open because it drifted into a compromise position that attracted rebels to its pews, but only the most conservative of them.

Thus, New Castle would be divided between rebel radicals and conservatives, as well as those loyal to the king. While the Presbyterian meetinghouse led the radical path for independence, Immanuel was more neutral, like the churches of the two counties south of New Castle, where loyalism made a strong appearance. Immanuel had the conservative rebels, such as George Read and its pastor, Aeneas Ross, the son of first rector. Ross avoided personally saying prayers for the king by inviting other clergymen to do it. Immanuel's leaders were slow to support independence; typically, Read opposed the Declaration of Independence in early July 1776, although he did sign the document in August with many others. At least thirty-four of Immanuel's members joined the New Castle County militia, and some of them actually served. The church had loyalists, but it was not dominated by them; rather, conservative rebels spoke for it.

The diversity of opinion at Immanuel can be indicated if we look at a few of its members. One of its leading rebels was James Booth. Born in 1753, he had a house on Delaware Street that he leased and then bought in 1794. It was the center of his extended family, including slaves and free blacks and members of Immanuel Church. It was conveniently located near the Courthouse, where Booth served in many capacities. He was secretary of both the Delaware Constitutional Conventions of 1776 and 1792. He was also the clerk of the assembly in the 1780s, served briefly in the Second Regiment of the New Castle County militia and was marshal of the admiralty court for the state of Delaware in New Castle, where prize vessels taken from the enemy were certified and sold. After the war, Booth filled a number of positions both in the navy and in the government of Delaware, as well as participated in the committee that established the boundaries of New Castle. He finally served as chief justice of Delaware, although he had no formal legal training. His holding of multiple offices subjected him to accusations of putting personal interests first and of being a secret loyalist.

Another member of Immanuel, Theodore Maurice, was a definite, yet beloved, loyalist. Born in England, Maurice came to Pennsylvania in 1754. Twelve years later, he had become chief clerk of the court of common pleas and register of probate and wills for New Castle County; four years later, he added the office of controller of His Majesty's customs in the port of New Castle. He "lived well and in an expensive way" on these combined incomes. In 1776, when he refused the assembly's offer to continue in the former two positions under the new government and his customs position lapsed, he became jobless. He surrendered the seal and his papers to the assembly in late February 1777.

When Maurice attended Immanuel Church, he had powerful friends among the conservative rebels, enough that he found that he could quietly remain in New Castle. His friends included Ann Clay Booth (sister of James Booth), whom Maurice had tutored; she thought of him fondly as an English gentleman. The Booth family kept Maurice's portrait in their dining room after he left New Castle. He was able to stay in New Castle until June 1778, when the British evacuated Philadelphia. By then, he felt that the king's government would not be restored. He was so respected in the community that when he prepared for his Atlantic voyage on a British ship, Delaware president Caesar Rodney ordered the local militia commander, Samuel Patterson, to provide Maurice with "sheep, fowls and other articles for his sea store." The county records of what was owed to Maurice were taken by the British in Wilmington, and he was never able to claim what was owed him.

George Read, the attorney and politician, was the most important member of Immanuel. He was born in Maryland in 1733, but when he was very young, his family moved to Christina, Delaware. He attended Alison's Presbyterian Academy and was admitted to the Pennsylvania Bar in 1753. A year later, he moved to New Castle and married Gertrude, the daughter of Immanuel's rector George Ross, and they attended Immanuel Church. Before the Revolutionary War, he was an assemblyman and Crown attorney general for the Three Lower Counties. When hostilities broke out, he, along with McKean, represented Delaware in the Continental Congresses. Unlike McKean, he was conservative, supporting the reconciliation policy of the Delaware Assembly, voting at first against independence for the colonies. He remained friends with McKean, even though his politics were much more restrained.

Engraving by Samuel Sartain, after 1860 painting by Thomas Sully, of George Read Sr. In 1754, Read Sr. moved to New Castle, married Gertrude, the daughter of Immanuel Church's rector, George Ross, and attended Immanuel Church. He represented Delaware in the Continental Congresses. He was conservative, supporting the reconciliation policy of the Delaware Assembly and voting at first against independence for the colonies, yet in August, he signed the Declaration of Independence. *Courtesy Wikimedia Commons.*

Despite the variety of opinion at Immanuel, rebels from outside New Castle were suspicious of all Anglican churches. In explaining the disaffection of loyalists in Delmarva Peninsula in March 1777, Brigadier General William Smallwood of Maryland claimed that religion was "the original cause" of the disaffection from the rebel cause and that the greatest number "conceal their true motives and make religion a cloak for their nefarious designs." He felt that the Anglican Church was being used to hide loyalists. Immanuel's difficult compromise, orchestrated by Aeneas Ross, came to an end when he died in 1782, and the pulpit was vacant for more than a year until ex-Jesuit Charles Wharton was lured to the position. It remained to be seen what Immanuel would do in New Castle's postwar years.

Overall, the war was a burden for most congregations. Some were led by their pastors to form companies of militia and go into battle, with their pastor as leader. New Castle's Presbyterian Church came close to that ideal, but Montgomery chose to be chaplain to a statewide Continental regiment. Other congregations were divided, most with disastrous results, requiring revivals to restore a measure of harmony. Immanuel was unique in that its doors stayed open despite internal factions. Most Anglican churches had to close their doors as their priests refused to observe Congress's thanksgiving days and would not give up prayers for the king. With all their limitations, houses of worship were the places of greatest influence in deciding whether one would support or oppose independence.

The Assembly, Courts and Committees

In an indirect way, eighteenth-century New Castle was involved in Atlantic shipping and exposed to the regulatory influence of the Navigation Acts and parliamentary taxation in ports. New Castle was a port where trade and political ideas were influenced by events in nearby Philadelphia. At the beginning of the century, New Castle had a small customshouse, and its ships traded in Atlantic waters as far as the West Indies and the British Isles. However, Philadelphia easily eclipsed New Castle in Atlantic trade, and by the time of the Revolution, New Castle's trade was relegated to small coastal craft that chiefly connected with Philadelphia. This trade connection provided New Castle with income as it supplied ships sailing from Philadelphia. While they were loaded with merchandise at Philadelphia, they held off their final preparations for the voyage until they stopped at New Castle. Here they took on food and water for the voyage (especially animals for meat), added a few sailors and completed repairs. In this way, New Castle remained a port with a customshouse that became the scene of lively protest in the mid-1760s.

Following the ideals expressed in Dickinson's *Letters From a Farmer in Pennsylvania*, the Delaware Assembly meeting at New Castle's Courthouse would protest the efforts of Parliament to tax the colonies. In 1765, the Stamp Act crisis spread, as Parliament required that paper documents have a stamp, and a few residents, like Thomas McKean, were designated to collect stamp revenue, although he never exercised the unpopular office. Because no colonial assembly had consented to this tax, when the ship with the stamps arrived before New Castle, the captain feared that a crowd would destroy them and thus decided not to unload them. Delaware's assembly had appointed a Committee of Correspondence whose members wrote to other places on how to oppose the Stamp Act. In February 1766, when the courts met at New Castle, the grand jury refused to act unless the courts disregarded the requirements of the Stamp Act, and the business of the courts was conducted without using the stamps. Parliament repealed the Stamp Act in a matter of months, and New Castle was illuminated by candle and bonfire to celebrate the repeal. In 1769, the New Castle County Grand Jury objected to the Townshend Duties on several commodities, of which the most notorious was tea, and freeholders met at nearby Christiana Bridge to protest.

OPPOSITION TO ROYAL GOVERNMENT

In neighboring Maryland and Virginia, the wealthy planter class that dominated their legislatures led the opposition to Parliament's effort to tax the colonies and the effort to create a new government. In New Castle County, conditions were a bit different. As we have seen, New Castle held most of Delaware's planters in the hundreds surrounding it. But they were never as numerous or as wealthy as those in Virginia, for they had to share political power with two other interest groups, attorneys and merchants. The former were at home in New Castle where the legislature met and the courts functioned. They claimed superiority in status to the merchants because they were disinterested patriots not driven by personal gain in trade. The merchants were the middlemen between the farmers and the task of processing and marketing their crops, as they often owned the mills where grain was ground and shipped. The best of them participated in coastal trade, chiefly with Philadelphia. Of course, there was some overlapping in the occupations, as most of the successful elite sought to invest in land and thus were inclined to farm at some stage in their lives. With the possible exception of Dover Hundred, the rest of state could not produce such a mixed leadership.

Early committees of protest were created in response to the formation of and calls from the Continental Congress and thus operated outside of the existing Delaware government dominated by the assembly. In June 1774, five hundred people were gathered by Thomas McKean on New Castle's Green to protest the Intolerable Acts that had closed the port of Boston and to listen to a prepared two-hour speech by McKean. He introduced seven points that were evidently supported by the crowd. It was resolved to form the New Castle

County Committee of Correspondence, headed by McKean, to respond to the crisis. It was to gather funds for the relief of the poor in Boston. The soliciting of funds or produce for Boston demonstrated a tie between New Castle's and Boston's Independence movements. The committee was also to lay the groundwork for a proposed meeting of the assembly in New Castle. Attorney George Read was also there, and he claimed that "not a sign of dissent appeared." Serving on the committee until completion of its effort in 1775 were New Castle's McKean, Read, Nicholas Van Dyke and Dr. George Munro, while other members were future militia commander Samuel Patterson of Christiana and merchant John Latimer of Newport. McKean and Van Dyke led in the collection of the Boston fund.

The meeting also initiated a call to the adjourned assembly to come to New Castle to elect delegates to the first Continental Congress in Philadelphia. McKean immediately sent a copy of his points to Kent and Sussex Counties, indicating that they represented the views of the freeholders and inhabitants of New Castle County. As expected, the assembly's representatives to Congress were McKean and Read of New Castle and Caesar Rodney of Kent County. Here was the first of several mobilized meetings of New Castle's community in which a popular throng was orchestrated to support the views of the protest leaders.

Later in the year, Congress requested the formation of vigilance committees to enforce boycotts and nonimportation policies. In November 1774, the New Castle Committee of Inspection was formed of members elected in each hundred, and it met at the New Castle Courthouse a month later. They approved the measures recommended by Congress, began the creation of a militia under their control and recommended that no ewes or lambs be killed during the next year. This last item was meant to support the growth of herds so that home-produced woolen cloth would replace that imported from Britain. It shows how extensively the county committees interpreted their powers even before the bloodshed at Lexington and Concord.

After word arrived of the clash between British troops and minutemen, concern for the further development of militia surfaced. Dissatisfied with funding for the militia in May 1775, New Castle's Committee of Inspection, its justices of the peace and its grand jury came together to recommend to the levy court a tax from each taxable inhabitant according to the county rates. The funds were to be paid to the committee to support the militia. Subcommittees in each hundred would force the many wavering taxpayers to support Congress. It must be remembered that such a taxation plan was radical in that it did not appear in the two lower counties.

The assembly was still divided on the issuing of arms to the inhabitants, let alone independence. Early in 1776, on their way to attend a meeting of the assembly, in which they represented Sussex County, Thomas Robinson and Boaz Manlove were arrested by a light infantry company in Dover as suspected loyalists. Robinson had actually been a member of a local committee of correspondence. Attorney and acting governor George Read got them released on the basis "breach of legislative privilege," an act that those who favored independence claimed encouraged loyalism. Later, Robinson and Manlove would become leading loyalists in Sussex County. Read's action made him appear to be more conservative than most of his colleagues in New Castle County.

In mid-June 1776, McKean came from his power base in Congress to the assembly at the courthouse and asked the members to establish a new government. Prior to this, he and the assembly's other delegates to Congress had been instructed that reconciliation with the mother country was the highest priority. This time, though, the assembly was willing to produce separation documents that unanimously declared Delaware to be independent of Pennsylvania. Although William Penn had created the existing assembly in 1704, the executive had remained in the hands of the Penn family so that the assembly now swept away the Penn family's still existing proprietary authority. In New Castle, this event would be as revolutionary as the Declaration of Independence.

The assembly's separation documents were still halfway measures in terms of independence because the representatives sent to Congress were not required to support independence from Britain and because the personnel of the new Delaware government remained the king's appointments until a new Delaware constitution could be written. Thus, New Castle's Richard McWilliam, appointed chief justice by the Crown in 1773, remained in that position until 1777. Meanwhile, in Philadelphia, the Declaration of Independence was written, and on July 24, 1776, public presentation of the document was made in front of the Courthouse before a crowd and militia mobilized to represent the community, which then destroyed the symbols of the British monarchy that were still attached to the exterior of the building.

Finally, at the Courthouse in late August, the Delaware convention, dominated by New Castle's George Read, began work on a new state constitution. It would be a cumbersome document whose chief feature was to continue the dominance of the colonial assembly at the expense of the executive and the judiciary. Checks and balances were there on paper, but in reality the assembly continued to rule. Members of the assembly were elected annually, seven from each county, from a franchise of freeholders owning fifty acres of land, twelve of it improved or otherwise being worth forty pounds.

A bicameral legislature was made up of the assembly and the Legislative Council. The new office of president and commander in chief was created, but he was elected by the legislature for a three-year term and had no veto power. Although commander in chief, he could only call up the militia with the consent of the four-man Privy Council. This body, appointed by the legislature, further checked what little power the position had. Election laws continued as they had been previously. Without naming a religious denomination, the document required that officeholders believe in the Trinity and the divine inspiration of Holy Scripture. The new constitution was far from being a revolutionary document, aiming to make the assembly, not Congress or the local committees, the dominant authority.

One of the reasons the constitution looked like what already existed is that some members of the convention were loyalists. At least two of the delegates from Sussex County were avowed loyalists. The elections that followed to chose the assembly in October were tumultuous, as loyalists and rebels contended with one another. In Lewes, Sussex County's seat, on election day a mob of six hundred cut down the liberty pole and ruled the streets with shouts of "Huzza for King George!" Beatings and insults from both sides were clearly meant to influence voting. The violent elections upset conservative rebels and showed that the independence movement had yet to build a consensus in Delaware.

What went on at the Courthouse in debating these issues is not always revealed. Pennsylvania loyalist George Galloway claimed that "[t]here was throughout the war a majority of the [Delaware] Assembly in favor of retaining their allegiance [to Britain], but it was a small government surrounded by larger ones and incapable of acting of itself." The majority of representatives who favored Britain were from Kent and Sussex Counties, not New Castle. Since the three counties' populations were almost equal, and representation in voting was equal, the two lower counties could inevitably outvote New Castle County.

In 1776, Washington's army had been unable to defend New York City from General William Howe's forces, which would occupy the city for the rest of the war. Things looked bleak to John Dickinson, who had retired to his Delaware estate after failing to head off the Declaration of Independence. There, on December 16, 1776, he wrote to his friend, George Read, indicating that "[t]his winter is the only time that will be allowed to us to think of peace before we suffer indescribable calamities." While the Declaration of Independence had been signed, Dickinson was still not reconciled to independence from the English Constitution he revered.

THE GOVERNMENT LEAVES NEW CASTLE

Delaware's two lower counties, Kent and Sussex, had always resented New Castle's role as capital. They were more reluctant to seek independence and felt pushed by New Castle's powerful Independence movement when meetings were held there. As early as 1774, when McKean suggested that the assembly convene at New Castle to elect representatives to the Continental Congress, it was known that the people of Sussex County "greatly disapprove of New Castle as the place of…the Assembly's meeting." While McKean would be elected to the convention that wrote Delaware's new constitution, his ally, Caesar Rodney, would not be, and even McKean, along with Rodney, failed to be sent back to Congress by the government elected under the new constitution. It was as if they were being reprimanded for having supported independence in July 1776. Over the objection of McKean, the conservatives convinced the assembly to move from New Castle, first to Newark and eventually to the more central Dover, the inland seat of Kent County.

When Howe prepared to capture Philadelphia in September 1777, Delaware authorities emphasized a further need to abandon New Castle because as a Delaware coastal port, the cattle grazing in its meadows and marsh could fall into enemy hands. This policy of moving the government away from New Castle proved to be a disaster, as the first location, Newark, turned out to be directly in Howe's path, for he chose to come by way of Chesapeake Bay, landing in Maryland at Head of Elk. He advanced on Newark, devastating it on his march, causing the loss of some of the assembly's papers, although most had been moved. Howe then marched on to the Cooch's Bridge area, opposed partially by the New Castle County militia, its first confrontation with the British army.

What Was It Like to Go to War

The administration of Delaware's war effort in September 1775 fell to a Committee of Safety that was formed by leaders from Delaware's three counties. It confirmed the appointment of militia officers, drafted regulations for the units and raised supplies to meet Congressional requests. In January 1776, its membership from New Castle County included James Latimer, Gunning Bedford Sr., Nicholas Van Dyke and George Read. When the new constitution was drafted in September, the convention continued the Delaware Council of Safety, now designated to function when the legislature was not in session. It would have difficulty with rival authorities like Congress, which also wanted to direct how Delaware's military resources would be used.

Militia

The Lower Three Counties militia had been established during the colonial wars. As noted, the Committees of Inspection recommended by Congress had met at New Castle's Courthouse in December 1774 and began reviving the militia, consisting of all men ages sixteen to fifty. Each soldier had to have a firelock, a bayonet, half a pound of powder, two rounds of lead, a cartouch box or powder horn and a bag of balls. In March 1775, the militia officers met and organized the units more formally. More than any other organization, the independence leaders sought to control the militia by dominating the Committees of Inspection. It was their activity that brought New Castle directly into the War for Independence.

Uniforms of the Lower, Middle and Upper Division Regiments of the New Castle County Militia, 1775. *Company of Military Historians, 1982.*

A list of New Castle taxpayers for 1776 shows that eighty of them would be enlisted in the Second Regiment of New Castle County militia. No blacks appeared because they, apprentices and indebted servants were exempt from mustering, a condition that would basically remain throughout the war. Samuel Patterson of Christiana, a miller, slaveholder and Presbyterian, was the regiment's colonel. Even those with loyalist leanings mustered when pressured by the authorities, although they deserted as quickly as possible. In fact, two captains of the New Castle County militia, Jacob Derickson and Joshua North, both from Brandywine Hundred, would become notorious loyalists.

As a numerous body, the militia had potential voting clout. When in late 1776 the assembly was writing the new constitution and setting elections, McKean endeavored to postpone the elections until Haslet's and Patterson's regiments, which he noted were away risking their lives for their country, could participate. McKean's defeat on the issue told him that conservatives wanted to control the new government and feared the votes of troops with strong egalitarian convictions. However, New Castle's militia would never be the political force that McKean experienced with Philadelphia's militia. There, militia grievances and mutiny were the rule, and the seizing and looting of loyalist families was its favorite pastime, while it was almost totally incompetent on the battlefield.

In truth, after Montgomery rallied this militia at New Castle in 1775, the men were not much used as there was no British enemy at hand and farmers needed their sons for the harvest. Congress called up five hundred Delaware militia in December 1776 to serve six weeks as it looked like the British would seize Philadelphia. The Council of Safety hesitated to act, although three companies of New Castle County militia, under Major Thomas Duff, did respond. They marched toward and arrived in Philadelphia but did not see action in Washington's army at nearby Trenton and Princeton. Members of Congress itself fled to Baltimore, forcing member Dr. Benjamin Rush and his wife to visit his sister, Rachel Montgomery, in New Castle, from which Rush went on alone to unpleasant accommodations in Baltimore.

In May and June 1777, the Delaware militia was again called out by Congress for what turned out to be false alarms. Finally in August, three New Castle County regiments under Colonels Thomas Duff, Samuel Patterson and Richard Cantwell turned out, all together a peak of 1,075 men. As we have seen, Samuel Patterson's Second Regiment was New Castle's.

Problems with the militia surfaced quickly. While some men did go to Philadelphia at the request of Congress late in 1776, after that the New Castle County militia would only defend its own territory, refusing to appear at a mustering of state militia in Kent County, even though it was called by President Caesar Rodney. Furthermore, militia turnout declined after the August 1777 peak. When the wealthy Captain John Clark summoned his New Castle company to meet Howe's army, only a minority was prepared to march and a quarter refused to follow him. Still, about one-third did march with Patterson to Cooch's Bridge, where they joined Ulster-born Brigadier General William Maxwell's Continental light infantry. They opposed the vanguard of Howe's army on September 3 at the bridge, where they stood up to the enemy, contributing to a stiff fight, although Howe was able to brush them aside. In the four days between the Battle of Cooch's Bridge and the Battle of the Brandywine, British captain William Dansey captured a horse, arms, drums and baggage, along with the distinctive Delaware militia flag. It appears that the flag belonged to Colonel Samuel Patterson's Second Regiment recruited in New Castle.

When Washington attempted to block Howe at Brandywine, he was defeated, suffering more than 1,200 bloody casualties. The British success demoralized the New Castle County militia, and by the end of September, the men had melted away. A month later, the Delaware Council of State felt that, at best, 300 New Castle County militia could be called up, less than one-third of what had mustered only four months before.

THE FLYING CAMP

New Castle taxpayers sent 5 to 8 men to the flying camp in Perth Amboy, New Jersey, in the second half of 1776. The small number was wise, for the camp had an unsavory reputation and a brief existence. In March 1776, faced with defending an expansive territory in the middle colonies from British operations, Washington had recommended forming a "flying camp," which referred to a mobile, strategic reserve of troops. Congress agreed and, on June 3, 1776, passed a resolution "that a flying camp be immediately established in the middle colonies and that it consist of 10,000 men." The recruits were to be militiamen from three colonies: 6,000 from Pennsylvania, 3,400 from Maryland and 600 from Delaware and were to serve until December 1, 1776. They were to be paid and fed in the same manner as regular soldiers of the Continental army. Brigadier General Hugh Mercer of Virginia was named commandant, while Samuel Patterson commanded a small New Castle contingent. As foreseen, the militia would stay only for a month rather than until the end of the year, so the camp experienced high desertion rates and even munity on the part of the politicized Philadelphia militia. Thomas McKean commented on the Philadelphia battalion he commanded that it consisted of "some of the most rude, turbulent, impudent, dirty fellows" he had ever seen. Joseph Booth, James's brother, of the Second Regiment, was able to get his nephew-apprentice out of the camp because he claimed that he was needed for work in the tannery at home. The flying camp disappeared at the end of the year, although the units from it had served at the Battles of Long Island and White Plains.

The Delaware Whig Battalion

To counteract the malaise caused by Howe's conquest of Philadelphia, on October 17, 1777, Thomas McKean, acting president of Delaware, with the consent of two members of the Privy Council (the others having fled to New Jersey), introduced a plan to freshly raise only six hundred militiamen, who were dubbed the Delaware Whig Battalion. New Castle County was to contribute three hundred, the other two counties making up the difference. The approach was far more realistic than earlier musters. Recruits would be asked to serve for only two months, and the battalion did not have to leave the state but rather would defend Delaware now that the British occupied Philadelphia. Each soldier was to provide a musket and blanket, and if those were lacking, they should be taken from disaffected loyalists, justified by the policy of disarming their enemies. Further, "if levies cannot be procured, any volunteers from any place whatsoever were to be received." Samuel Patterson was designated brigadier general, while George Craighead of Brandywine Hundred was his lieutenant colonel; the captains were James Black, John James, Thomas Watson, Isaac Lewis, William Moody and William Rankin. The rest of the militia—with the exceptions of one company in disaffected Sussex County and a temporary guard when the assembly convened at Dover—was disbanded. Of the proposed companies, James Black's, John James's, Thomas Watson's and Isaac Lewis's were formed, but they were much understrength. In November, Lewis's company was able to raid the loyalist strongholds on Duck Creek. This was the only action before the battalion's enlistments expired.

Reviewing the captains of the Whig Battalion, typical was James Black of Mill Creek Hundred in New Castle County, a Scots-Irishman from Londonderry. Born in 1736, four years later he immigrated with his family to the Eastern Shore of Maryland. In the early 1770s, he moved to Mill Creek Hundred, where his first and second wives died. In 1777, on the basis of his militia record, he was elected to serve in the Delaware Assembly at Dover, operating under the new constitution. A year later, he was named a justice of the peace but did not return to the assembly, preferring instead to practice law. After the war, in 1785, he was appointed to the four-man Privy Council, which was a check on the president. In 1793, he went back to Dover as member of the state House of Representatives, where his term was cut short by his death a year later. The practice of the law and his service in the militia were steppingstones to a political career.

DELAWARE'S CONTINENTAL REGIMENT

New Castle's 1776 taxpayers joined this constantly renewed Continental regiment in much greater numbers than the flying camp, twenty-seven of them serving in Haslet's or, later, Hall's Continental Regiment. Presbyterian Scots-Irishmen were numerous in the regiment. Its first colonel, John Haslet, had been an ordained Presbyterian minister in Ulster, although he gave up the vocation when he settled in 1757 in Kent County, where he served in the militia during the Seven Years' War. He was a supporter of Caesar Rodney and the Independence movement. Raised in the spring of 1776, his Continental regiment was at first detailed to oppose Delaware loyalists. However, it became part of Washington's army and was annually recruited and placed in the most dangerous positions, in actions where defeats outnumbered victories. Haslet was killed in December 1776 at the Battle of Princeton, where much of the regiment was wiped out. He was replaced by Captain David Hall of Sussex County, who was made colonel in April 1777. Hall commanded the regiment at both Brandywine and Germantown, but he was wounded in the latter battle and needed a long recuperation, delaying his return to the regiment. In 1780, he refused to go with the regiment when it was sent to South Carolina. Later commanders of the regiment were Joseph Vaughan and Robert Kirkwood. The list of service outside of Delaware is impressive: Long Island, White Plains, Trenton, Princeton, Brandywine, Germantown, Monmouth, Camden, Cowpens, Guilford Court House, Hobkirk's Hill, Siege of Ninety-Six, Eutaw Springs and Yorktown. During most of the war, the regiment's appearance in Delaware was limited to recruiting.

Private Haslet's Delaware Continental Regiment, pre-1779. *Company of Military Historians, 1982.*

The Continental regiment appeared in New Castle on July 24, 1776, to celebrate the Declaration of Independence with bonfires on the Green, started with royal portraits from the courthouse. New Castle County militia officer and resident of Front Street Gunning Bedford Sr. had been named second in command of the regiment as Haslet's lieutenant colonel. Bedford was born in 1742 into a farm family in New Castle Hundred. His great-grandfather, William Bedford, had come to Delaware from Virginia, a descendant of an original Jamestown settler and a slaveholder like the Reads. He was educated at the College of Philadelphia. As a Continental officer, Bedford found that more of his men were sick and unfit than ready for duty. He was detached from his regiment in July to serve as deputy muster master for the Continental army being organized by Major General Philip Schuyler above Albany for the invasion of Canada. With his connections in Congress, he was able to assure Schuyler of their full support for the invasion, which Congress regarded as a pet project.

In late October, Bedford returned to his regiment and was wounded at the Battle of White Plains, and while he recovered, he slept on the ground for days with no blanket in chilly December. He complained to his influential brother-in-law, George Read, who got him blankets. After a year of action, when the regiment was renewed with most of the same officers, he declined further service and went home to conveniently take loyalist Theodore Maurice's old position as chief clerk of the court of common pleas. In 1779, he was admitted to the Delaware Bar. He had become a politician, not sharing in the regiment's further glory.

The Continental Army and County Militia

The British army under Howe had taken Philadelphia with relative ease, showing its superiority as a fighting force. In October 1777, exiled from his Philadelphia home, Dr. Benjamin Rush—surgeon general of the Middle Department of the Continental army and Joseph Montgomery's brother-in-law—noted that the British camps and medical facilities also contributed to their ability to win battles. He wrote to fellow Congressman John Adams about the contrast between the British and the rebel armies he had witnessed during Howe's effort to take his native city. Rush compared "the extreme regard our enemies pay to discipline, order, economy and cleanliness among their soldiers" with the Continental system formed for gain by the supposedly corrupt director general of hospitals, rather than "for the benefit of the sick and wounded." The British army had been warned against the spread of disease in blankets, had made a firm effort to procure vegetables for their men, appreciated the effectiveness of their surgeons and orderlies and had the presence of nightly guards to prevent "their men from contracting and prolonging distempers by rambling, drinking, and whoring." Rush was certainly a critic of the conditions in Washington's camps, perhaps unfairly, for the situation was beyond the commander in chief's resources or ability to control. Regardless, the contrast remained.

After 1777, the Delaware militia was too undependable to coordinate with Washington's army, and for the rest of the war, the men's duties were chiefly limited to policing loyalists within the state; monitoring Anglican, Methodist and Lutheran clergy; and preventing trade with the enemy. The militia was unable to answer Washington's pleas to support his army in nearby New Jersey. Instead, Caesar Rodney, president of Delaware, who worked with militia, begged Congress for even a small corps of Continentals because "they can be more effective than all the militia in the state." He complained that the militiamen were too close to their homes and insisted on returning there at night, the time when they were most needed. However, in the summer of 1780, some militia under Lieutenant Colonel Henry Neill did leave the state to serve in northern New Jersey and at Dobb's Ferry on the Hudson River. Still, the state's highest military priority was to sustain its Continental regiment, which saw heavy service in other states.

Military leadership also was a problem. Haslet was killed at the end of 1776, and his replacement, David Hall, failed to serve after 1778 because of wounds. The realities of camp life and command forced Gunning Bedford to retire from the Delaware Continentals after only a year of service. Thomas McKean never again served as a soldier after his experience with militia at the flying camp and would permanently retire from Delaware politics in 1779. While they supported the rebel cause, the enthusiasm of these early leaders for military service had certainly dampened by 1778.

The failure of the Delaware militia to turn out after 1777 displays the weakness of the militia system. The militiamen's conduct in policing loyalists often showed them at their worst because they were prone to vandalism, indiscriminate destruction, fulfillment of personal grudges and, on rare occasions, assassination. With all of its deficiencies, however, the militia played a role, if a diminished one, as the civil war continued.

Howe's Occupation

When he was in New York, Lieutenant General William Howe had made it a point of honor that he sought loyalist support, and he proclaimed a policy of pacification and reconciliation when he invaded rebel territory. With this in mind, he had decided to capture Philadelphia in the summer of 1777. On August 27, just after his army had landed near Head of Elk, he issued a proclamation to the peaceable inhabitants of Pennsylvania, Delaware and Maryland. He offered a pardon to residents who had taken up arms against the king if they would voluntarily surrender themselves to the king's troops. Here was a tempting offer, especially for the disaffected among the militia being gathered to oppose him.

The Delaware Estuary would be spared when Howe's fleet took the longer route, moving up the Chesapeake Bay to Head of Elk to advance on Philadelphia. His 267 vessels not only included Royal Navy warships but also, in their wake, New York privateers and a few loyalist raiders. As the fleet moved north on the Chesapeake, they were welcomed by blacks who tried to swim to them. Not until they landed unopposed at Elk Ferry were they off the ships that had left New York. They advanced on land, while Maryland and Delaware militia tried to interrupt their forage parties and prevent desertions of slaves and white servants to them. After Philadelphia fell to Howe on September 26, he occupied the city, and loyalist bands operated more openly.

Still, a few weeks later, Howe sent most of the Royal Navy back to the Delaware River to penetrate northward toward Philadelphia's naval defenses. While he held Philadelphia, he still had to capture the river forts to the south

Mezzotint, published in London in 1777, of Lieutenant General William Howe. A brilliant tactician, Howe was slow to take advantage of his many victories and was accused of harboring hopes of reconciliation long after it was possible.

of the city so that the Royal Navy could supply the city and his army. Kent County authorities reacted by posting two militia companies to stop black slaves from flocking to the enemy ships, trying to prevent what had happened previously on the Chesapeake. By October 11, the British fleet reached New Castle. Two days later, George Read, who had escaped from Philadelphia for Salem, New Jersey, crossed the Delaware River with his family, including his mother and infant children. His landing was not without incident, since the tide was out and his small craft became stuck in the mud flats without making the shore. British tars in a barge, unaware of Read's identity, came to their rescue and unloaded the boat with its precious cargo on the shore.

Over the next year, New Castle would be confronted by the Royal Navy, which held the Delaware River in front of the town. Within a few days, sixty New Castle militia seized three or four British sailors who had come ashore. New Castle, however, would not be bombarded or garrisoned as had Wilmington; in fact, a relatively cordial relationship developed. Royal Navy personnel visited the town to obtain water and supplies and enjoy the pleasures of being on land, while in exchange the ships sold New Castle's citizens valuable salt. The town became more loyalist and neutral, as many prominent rebels like George Read decided not to stay, closing their houses and, in his case, sending his family to the supposed inland safety of Maryland.

Mezzotint of Sir Andrew Hamond by George Henry Phillips, after Sir Thomas Lawrence, published in 1830 by Martin Colwaghi. Captain of the HMS *Roebuck*, Hamond patrolled the Delaware Estuary from 1776 on and rendezvoused with Howe's fleet on July 1777, whereupon Hamond recommended that Howe continue north, even to New Castle. Howe, instead, chose to capture Philadelphia by way of Chesapeake Bay.

The Royal Navy went on to besiege and take Philadelphia's Forts Mifflin, Mercer and Red Bank, the former being abandoned by the rebels on November 16. Two days before, a fleet of six ships of the line, two frigates and galley began a fierce cannonade of Fort Miffin that led Continental private Joseph Plumb Martin to comment, "If ever destruction was complete, it was here." The other bulwark of Philadelphia's defense was Pennsylvania's fleet, commanded by Commodore John Hazelwood, consisting of a frigate, a brig, a schooner, thirteen row galleys and numerous fire ships and rafts. Hazelwood's schooner *Delaware* ran aground, where it was set on fire by the British, a demonstration that was soon repeated until much of the Pennsylvania fleet was burned or abandoned. By the spring of 1778, the Pennsylvania navy had ceased to defend the Delaware Estuary because it no longer existed. The Royal Navy now ruled the Delaware River.

With the British in Philadelphia supplied by the Delaware River, New Castle was placed at the front lines of the war. A description of the place in October 1777 by Howe's secretary and loyalist pamphleteer, Ambrose Serle, shows that while it was surrounded by a rich agricultural area, "the principle houses…are utterly abandoned by the inhabitants on account of their concern in the rebellion." He went on: "[T]here being no wharf or dock, where ships can ride out the strong current, it does not seem probable that this town will ever grow." Serle continued to describe the town's courthouse and [jail], the Presbyterian and Anglican houses of worship and "a pound for hogs." It can be assumed that the town's dilapidated state was the result of rebel leaders leaving and the disruption of trade, as their resources had been expended against Howe's invasion.

During the British occupation of coastal Delaware in October 1777, McKean was asked to head the state government because President McKinly had been captured by the British and George Read was still not in Delaware. McKean felt that he was being asked "to save a poor and distressed state without a head, without a shilling, public records & papers in possession of the enemy, together with their capital & principal trading town; the militia dispirited and dispersed, many of them fled out of the state for safety, and the majority of the rest supposed to be disaffected from the glorious cause we are engaged in." This is when he formed the Whig Battalion. Howe's occupation of Philadelphia would continue to negatively affect Delaware.

Loyalists would be influential in New Castle until the British evacuation in June 1778. Earlier, McKean had outlined what groups he felt were potential loyalists. He argued that the colonial Delaware and Pennsylvania political systems were corrupt because they gave the Quaker descendants of William Penn too much political power in relation to their numbers. McKean also saw the opposition to independence as being made up of Quakers, Mennonites, Anglicans and officers of the Crown and proprietors. They became loyalists, he argued, chiefly under the influence of Anglican missionaries, who were spreading the word that the rebellion was a plot by Presbyterians to get their church established. His opinion helps to identify New Castle's loyalists, who could be found on every level of society.

Theodore Maurice has already been mentioned as one of New Castle's leading loyalists. While the fleet was before New Castle, Maurice visited the Royal Navy ships and was asked to provide intelligence, but he thought himself under parole to the rebels and thus gave very little. His conduct showed him to be, in the words of Richard Penn, "a gentleman of the strictest probity and integrity."

Another loyalist was Dr. John Watson, a former Royal Navy surgeon who had emigrated from Scotland to America in 1767. At New Castle, he married a local girl and ran a prosperous physic surgery and apothecary. He reported that in the town he was mobbed for his loyalist sentiments, until he deserted the New Castle County militia and joined Howe's army at Head of Elk. At Aitkens Tavern, he gave information to Howe on the roads and nature of the country. In September 1777, he conducted Captain Patrick Ferguson's British riflemen on two excursions into the country. At the Brandywine River, the riflemen were under Lieutenant General Wilhelm Knyphausen, whose job was to tie down the rebel forces by crossing the Brandywine, as if he were Howe's entire army. He was opposed on the other side by rebels under the command of Brigadier General Maxwell who were to delay his advance, as they had been doing since the confrontation at Cooch's Bridge. Ferguson's riflemen performed well, and Maxwell was gradually forced back to the east bank, but they suffered heavy casualties. These included Ferguson, who was shot through the right elbow joint. He eventually recovered, although his right arm was permanently crippled. Watson became the badly needed surgeon for the riflemen corps at the Brandywine. With the British occupation, Watson went back to New Castle and became the leader of its loyalists, forming an association.

In another case, John Drake was born in Ireland and lived in New Castle from 1766, where he kept a public house and was employed at the Courthouse in the office for recording deeds. For urging allegiance to the Crown, he was forced to close his household in April 1776 and serve briefly in the county militia. However, he fled to Howe's army on the day of the Battle of Brandywine. On September 17, 1777, he was placed on the redoubtable Royal Navy ship *Roebuck*, where he served as a clerk in the sea service and quartermaster's department. As his wife attempted to board the *Roebuck* off New Castle with Mrs. Watson, she was shot in the neck by New Castle militia. When Philadelphia was evacuated, the Drakes went to New York, where he served in the navy Victualling Office.

With the evacuation in June 1778, Watson's Loyalist Association lost its support, and he and his wife and three children fled to the British vessels moored before New Castle. Watson was only able to take two chests, losing most of his personal belongings to the militia. He went to New York, where he served as a mate in the General Hospital. The presence of the Royal Navy at New Castle during the evacuation ensured that very few loyalists were left there.

As the British were leaving, the Delaware Assembly passed an Act of Free Pardon and Oblivion that forgave most loyalists but exempted the forty-six most notorious, twenty of whom were from New Castle County. The names from New Castle Hundred included Dr. John Watson, John Drake, John Greenwood (cooper), Thomas Nodes (cordwainer), Isaac Conner (cooper), Abraham Hackett (weaver) and Christian Smith (laborer). The dominance of craftsmen on the list reflects their role in outfitting Royal Navy ships.

The British invasion and occupation had momentarily made loyalism popular, but most loyalists had left New Castle with the British or remained on their best behavior, so their presence no longer seemed a threat. New Castle loyalists who left in 1778 would settle in New York, Nova Scotia or Britain. Immanuel may have lost most of its loyalists at this time, allowing it to survive for the duration of the war. Despite being targeted by the legislature as loyalists in the Act of Free Pardon, Christopher Wilson, William Almond and others simply gave bond and never left Delaware. Some estates were confiscated and sold, and part of the revenue was set aside to support the wives and children of exiled loyalists. Loyalists could petition the assembly to have their property restored. Thus, when the Peace of Paris was signed in 1783, New Castle County had only a few returning loyalists. In 1790, an act restored full citizenship to loyalists, although it did not treat property issues. Compared to other states, Delaware's government was not vindictive toward its loyalists.

Civil War from Coast to River

After the British left Philadelphia, New Castle County faltered in its ability to turn out militia and support the war. New Castle suffered a further decline in its coastal trade as loyalists and the Royal Navy cooperated to dominate the Delaware River. The former president of Delaware and one of New Castle's most important leaders, George Read, dropped out of politics. In 1779, he resigned from the Legislative Council and refused reelection to Congress, disappearing for over a year because of poor health. He built the substantial brick country house at Stonum, signifying the virtue of living in a retreat close to the soil. He did return modestly to the assembly in 1780 and, two years later, to the Legislative Council. He was also named a judge of the court of appeals in admiralty cases, a position that would put him in the middle of the continuing Delaware River civil war. Even after his return, he evidently was not well.

Loyalist Refugees

During October 1778, British war minister Lord George Germain made it clear that his support of loyalism also included the encouragement of loyalist privateers and military units. Royal Navy ships would back the loyalists. Thus, even after the British evacuated in 1778, the Delaware estuary and, more broadly, the Delmarva Peninsula remained possible British military objectives and continued to be torn by civil war. No more British armies would appear, but intense irregular warfare was carried on by loyalists, supported by a few Royal Navy ships and privateers from New York and Delaware. The coastal area was rich in tobacco, wheat and other grains, livestock and slaves, attracting not only the privateers but the commander of the Continental army as well. Washington looked at New Castle County's farms and plantations to support his hungry Continental army.

Welcoming the New York and Delaware privateers were indigenous loyalist raiders on Delaware's land and water called "refugees." Rebel authorities referred to them as such because it was assumed that they had been dislocated to undeveloped areas by economic conditions rather than a firm allegiance to the British Empire. This situation had begun before Howe invaded. In April 1777, Congress asked that livestock be removed from the vulnerable coast of Delaware, a policy that caused discord because it forced coastal farmers into Delaware's back country. Refugee raiding broke out in Sussex County, and the rebels felt they would lose their only foothold at Lewes. The Sussex refugees and loyalists were in easy contact with the loyalists on the Eastern Shore of Maryland, who had been named "picaroons" because of their casual depredations against rebel families and shipping. The picaroons, refugees and loyalists fed off one another and were often one in the same.

Delaware loyalist Cheney Chow, or "China Chow," ravaged Queen Anne and Kent Counties of the Eastern Shore. The raiders' practice "of landing in small parties and taking men out of their beds" was especially unnerving. While New Castle was not directly attacked, the fear of such activities made its inhabitants wary. As late as April 1781, Governor William Livingston of New Jersey added his state to the victims, noting that "those dirty pirates… hitherto have defied with impunity all the states reached by [the Delaware River]." Evidently, the rebels felt that these loyalist rovers were pirates.

During the British naval occupation of New Castle, Dr. John Watson and Thomas Slater, a Newport loyalist, had acted like refugees in making a contribution to the British war effort. They outfitted an armed row galley with twenty refugees at the oars to attack rebel shipping in the Delaware River. Watson took prisoners, including Robert Taylor, who was exchanged for a loyalist. An unfulfilled goal of the galley was to return to New Castle and make prisoners of the rebels who had opposed Watson. When it became evident that the British were evacuating Philadelphia, the galley was taken there to assist in the effort. But the Royal Navy confiscated it, and eventually it was destroyed by evacuating British sailors.

Already in April 1777, a British detachment from a ship patrolling near Lewes had taken runaway slaves and encouraged the numerous

Sussex County loyalists. Freedmen and slaves took the opportunity to board the British ships and ultimately leave with them for the liberty of New York. This was before Germain's policy, formally proclaimed a year later, asserted that blacks who deserted from an enemy master could follow any occupation they wished within the British lines. Still, since early in the war, when Virginia's Governor Dunmore had offered freedom to blacks who supported his army, slaves believed that the British army offered them greater opportunity for freedom and security than the Continental army.

The Assignment of the *Roebuck*

The loyalists and refugees needed the assistance of a few ships from the Royal Navy. In March 1776, Delaware Bay was patrolled by two Royal Navy ships, the *Roebuck* and the *Liverpool*, which Caesar Rodney called "pirates." Captain Andrew Snape Hamond of the *Roebuck* would have heartily disagreed with this assessment. Named for the small but agile deer of the British Isles, the *Roebuck* was laid down at Chatham Shipyard in 1770 and launched four years later as a prototype vessel, especially designed for North American waters. It was larger than the usual frigate, with two decks on which its forty-four guns were displayed. Yet it was small enough to operate in the shallow coastal waters of Delaware, where heavily armed ships of the line were often caught on shoals. The two ships were on His Majesty's business, although soon refugees and refugee barges and row galleys were joining them, making it appear as if they were all coastal raiders.

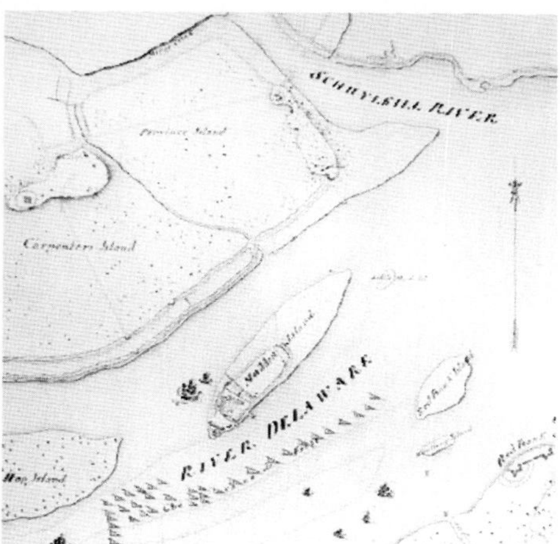

Map of the attack on Redbank (Fort Mercer), November 15, 1777. In the left corner are the *Liverpool*, *Pearl*, *Roebuck* and *Iris*. After five days' bombardment, the fort was abandoned by the rebels. *Courtesy Wikimedia Commons.*

The *Roebuck* and sister ship *Liverpool* had a remarkable and

Mezzotint of Andrew Snape Douglass, Captain of HMS *Roebuck* in the last years of the Revolutionary War. *Courtesy Wikimedia Commons.*

enduring assignment in the waters of the Delaware and Chesapeake Bays. In January 1776, the *Liverpool* was in Chesapeake Bay, while in March and April, the *Roebuck* cruised between Cape Henlopen and Lewes on the Delaware. In early May, the two frigates moved north to Reedy Island, forcing ammunition for Lewes to be sent overland. As they passed New Castle, they were confronted by rebel row galleys from Christiana, and the population turned out on both sides of the river to witness the two-day cannonade. The rebel galleys expended a great deal of ammunition, and the *Roebuck* was momentarily caught by a snag in the river but warded them off. The two warships continued no farther, but there was no direct combat.

Late in May, the *Roebuck* was sent to help Virginia's Governor Dunmore in Chesapeake Bay. It returned to New York in August with Dunmore as a passenger. There, in October, the *Roebuck* was in the fleet that sailed north of the city on the Hudson River, breaking through the boom that was to prevent further navigation. The *Roebuck* was back on the Delaware waters in April 1777, when it took two rebel war ships, the *Sachem* and the *Morris*. By September, the *Roebuck* and two other frigates had driven the rebel galleys from Wilmington, enabling the British to capture a sloop containing President John McKinly, the public records of Delaware and the treasury of New Castle County. Compared to this rich haul, the occupation of Wilmington was an afterthought. It was then that New Castle's John Drake was placed on the *Roebuck* as clerk. The *Roebuck* rendezvoused at the Delaware Capes with Howe's fleet on July 29, and Captain Hamond went aboard Howe's flagship, where he recommended that Howe continue and land at Reedy Island or even New Castle. As mentioned, Howe was not impressed.

The *Roebuck* continued its activities as the Royal Navy dominated the Delaware. In November 1777, it joined the *Liverpool*, *Pearl* and *Iris* in besieging Forts Mifflin and Mercer, participating in the bombardment of Fort Mercer that inflicted so many casualties that it was abandoned by the rebels on November 20, opening the way to Philadelphia. In January 1778, one of the *Roebuck*'s boats destroyed a rebel breastwork and captured two galleys on the New Jersey side of the Delaware River. Wherever it moved, it attracted loyalist refugees. The *Roebuck* was still present in 1781, guarding Cape Henlopen at the entrance to Delaware Bay, and off Virginia it took 290 prisoners when the USS *Confederacy* struck its colors. By this time, the *Roebuck* had a new commander: Hamond's eighteen-year-old nephew, Andrew Snape Douglas, who served on the frigate from 1775, becoming its lieutenant three years later and, early in 1780, its commander.

Civil War in the Forefront

After the British evacuated Philadelphia, the rebel government at Dover had difficulty in meeting the coastal challenge. The nature of this renewed war is seen in May 1778, when President Caesar Rodney reported to Thomas McKean that Dover was constantly alarmed by "the enemy and refugees," for seldom a day passed that people, especially along the bay, were taken off, and thus they were afraid to support the rebel cause "least they should be taken away and their houses plundered." He asked McKean to solicit Congress to underwrite a company of militia such as the three hundred raised on the Eastern Shore of Maryland to combat a similar situation. By August, Rodney claimed that the refugees "were on the coast from one end of the state to the other." The same month, Captain Silas Snow of the militia "was taken in the dead of night out of his warm bed by the refugees" and was soon languishing as a British prisoner on Long Island.

New Castle witnessed the rebels trying to retaliate against the coastal warfare with limited resources. Its port supported the rebel effort to free the Delaware waters of loyalist raiders. As mentioned, President McKean had organized and called up a Whig Battalion, and at least Isaac Lewis's company was able in November 1778 to march through Fair Neck to the Duck Creek area, south of New Castle. On Duck Creek, a loyalist stronghold, Lewis's men took several vessels. They sailed them to New Castle, where in June 1779 Marshal of Admiralty James Booth presided, declaring them prizes and selling them. Thus, Captain Lewis had a reward for appearing in the field.

In March 1779, the Pennsylvania Supreme Council, at the urging of Philadelphia's merchants, purchased the *General Greene* and gave it to Captain James Montgomery to patrol the Delaware. Accompanied by three Continental frigates, he sailed from Sandy Hook to the Virginia Capes. However, dissention among his sailors was so irate that he had to put down a mutiny and take prisoners. In June, Montgomery docked at New Castle, where he disembarked the mutineers (who were in shackles), as well as the enemy he had taken.

The refugees on water and land would also reduce the ability of Delaware to support its own militia and the Continental army. In August 1780, it was reported that two to three hundred loyalists had been raging about Sussex County, "[d]isarming the well effective, seizing the ammunition and refusing to pay their taxes…threatening destruction to all that should oppose them." All the parties sent out to spy on them had been taken prisoner. At the same time, the commissary at Lewes reported that supplies of corn and salt had come in very slowly. Earlier, effort had been made to collect supplies, wagons and horses to furnish Washington's Continental army. A year later, Washington himself begged for supplies from Delaware, but there were no funds to purchase such commodities.

By the fall of 1780, British admiral George Rodney reported to the admiralty that so many rebel ships of war and privateers had been taken by his ships that he held 1,400 prisoners, enough that "the rebels will find it extremely difficult to man the Continental ships of war now in the Delaware and at Boston." Not only had the British eliminated the Continental navy as a factor on the Delaware, but their harassment and blockade had also ruined the trade of the port of Philadelphia. After the British left Philadelphia, commerce at the port had come to a standstill, not just with ships bound for the Atlantic but in the coastal trade as well. Dependent as New Castle's wharfs were on Philadelphia's business, they must also have been empty. The situation would last beyond the war. With trade closed, the only way rebel merchants could make money for the rest of the war was to be involved in supplying the Continental army.

By 1781, Delaware authorities realized that their coast still had no protection and sought to build a navy and cooperate on the defense of the river with New Jersey. However, Governor William Livingston of New Jersey deflected the request to cooperate, stating that his militia in his three southern counties could operate on either land or water and thus New Jersey was prepared.

For a moment in April 1781, it looked like New Castle would again be involved in a British invasion of Delmarva. Intelligence came to Washington that Sir Henry Clinton would leave New York with a force to penetrate the Delaware River and make New Castle the center of his operations, encompassing the Delmarva Peninsula. In New York, Clinton had written of the need to make the Chesapeake and the Delaware a center of offensive action, "where the friends of the king were numerous." He had been inspired by the plans of Maryland's Kent County resident James Chambers, commander of the First Battalion of Maryland Loyalists, who had urged Clinton to send an expedition to occupy Delmarva. It would cut off supplies to Washington; destroy rebel strongholds like Baltimore and Annapolis; occupy Oxford, Head of Elk and Chestertown; and invade Virginia. Clinton soon received the support of Lord Charles Cornwallis on this effort, but when Cornwallis moved his army northward into Virginia, the expedition seemed less necessary.

In its usual defensive mode, Congress reacted to the threat by ordering its board of war in Philadelphia to enforce the removal of all public stores in the Delmarva Peninsula to prevent them from falling into enemy hands. Its commissary general was to move stores to safer places, and Delaware, Maryland and Virginia were asked to cooperate. Members of Congress claimed that they were doing this for the safety of Delmarva's citizens, but in reality, supplies were needed for the Continental army. All the activity came to naught. Clinton aborted the scheme, and the British never appeared before New Castle.

The loyalist refugees remained active. From Congress, Thomas Rodney wrote to his brother, Caesar, in April 1781 that Delaware flour and Indian corn was unprotected from the refugees because the state could not afford the craft to do this. In August, John Dickinson in Philadelphia received news that his Kent County plantation had been raided by "refugees consisting of 15 men and boys," confining his servants and plundering the house and kitchen of provisions, liquors, blankets, sheets, curtains and furniture, while the library was left untouched. They also asked the slaves to go with them, but evidently Dickinson was a good master, for all but one refused. News of the raid reached Dover, and sixty men went out, but the refugees escaped by the beach. Dickinson's losses totaled more than £1,500.

Also in August, the thirty-eight-gun Continental frigate *Trumbull*, the only surviving frigate of the original Continental navy, sailed out the Delaware River on a mission to Havana, Cuba, with dispatches and a cargo of flour to be exchanged for needed munitions. Lackluster Captain James Nicholson commanded it. A year earlier, Nicholson and the *Trumbull* had fought the bloodiest contest of their careers against a loyalist privateer, *Watt*, that ultimately escaped. Now, the *Trumbull* passed Lewes but was intercepted by the thirty-two-gun Royal Navy ship *Iris*, which contested the frigate's passage. In the contest, the *Trumbull* lost sixteen men killed and more wounded, striking its colors to the *Iris*. It was then discovered that the victorious British ship had originally been the *Hancock* of the Continental navy, which the British had renamed and refitted. Such was the feeble state of the Continental navy in the Delaware Estuary.

In September, Washington again passed through New Castle County on his way to Yorktown. He was following Howe's path in reverse. This route had evolved into a supply line for Washington's army after the British evacuated Philadelphia. A Continental commissary had been developed at Head of Elk to collect wheat, cattle and other supplies for distribution to the Continental army. From there, wagons transported the supplies to Christiania Bridge. Then most of them were shipped by water to Wilmington, although some went by wagon to New Castle. Once the supplies reached the Delaware River, they were shipped to Philadelphia and then points farther north on the river that was close to Washington's army. In this way, the produce of Delmarva came to Washington's army, and hence the area has been dubbed "the Breadbasket of the Revolution." However, it is also evident that this supply line was often interrupted by refugees, picaroons and British warships.

On October 19—the same day Lord Charles Cornwallis surrendered at Yorktown—the mind of Thomas Rodney, Caesar's brother, was on other concerns. He was continuing plans to pursue the destructive refugees in Delaware Bay and River and hoped that "effectual measures" would be taken "[t]o prevent the refugees from harassing our bay next summer." While Cornwallis's surrender at Yorktown was certainly significant in bringing the land war to a close, it had minimal effect on the civil war in Delaware and Chesapeake Bays.

In truth, the war in Delaware Bay continued into the summer of 1782. In March, refugee captain Roger Jones was caught in Philadelphia blatantly casing the port as to what vessels were leaving and the extent of their armament, with the expectation that they would become prizes. Royal Navy ships and privateers also continued to come out of New York to raid the area. On the Delaware waters, the British frigate *Medea* took nine merchantmen from Philadelphia. The *Medea* was a small, twenty-eight-gun ship that had been built at England's Plymouth Dockyard and commissioned in May 1778 under the command of Captain William Cornwallis. The French fleet, so crucial to the Yorktown campaign, had left for the West Indies, but the French army remained and had to be paid. In September, two French ships,

Gloire and *L'Aogle*, entered Delaware Bay with the army's payroll of 500,000 lire in gold. British warships attacked and took the two vessels, but not before French officers escaped to the shore with the payroll.

The civil war in Delaware continued to outdistance the fall of Yorktown. Loyalist refugees were still active in February and March 1783 as the Peace of Paris was being negotiated. At Duck Creek, the loyalist stronghold south of New Castle, the loyalists had a galley named *Lady's Revenge* that was taken by Captain Snyder, although the loyalist crew escaped. Nearby, Robert Appleton, constable of lower New Castle County, was seized by a loyalist party. Having discovered that Appleton was a Methodist, they ordered him to preach a Methodist sermon, and when he refused, they beat and whipped him with a thick rope. They destroyed his papers and made him promise not to serve the rebels. He was released on Duck Creek, and when he returned to his duties, he was again beaten. However, rebel militia under Captain Allen McLane retaliated against the loyalists, taking their vessels and scattering the crews in Cedar Swamp.

The rebels soon applied the term "pirate" to the refugees, loyalists or picaroons of Chesapeake and Delaware Bays. The implication of being a pirate carried them beyond the status of a privateer, in which a vessel held a letter of marque from a state authority to attack only enemies and to take prizes before an admiralty court, where the spoils were divided. In contrast, pirates could attack vessels of any nation and seize booty that was then directly distributed among the captain and crew. The disparaging title was given to refugee raiders because they sprang so quickly on their quarry and disappeared just as rapidly, the ideal of partisan war. It was the inability of rebel authorities to find and confront them that caused the frustration that led them to use the term "pirate."

Overall, after the British evacuation of Philadelphia in 1778, the civil war on the Delaware River and its tributaries continued in earnest. It was unvarnished war, full of the tragedy and destruction that had been warned about when the possibility of independence was debated earlier. During these years, New Castle suffered in several ways: it lost its role as capital of Delaware, its trade was ruined like that of Philadelphia by the British blockade, its two churches found it difficult to keep their doors open and even the productive countryside of New Castle Hundred was stripped in the effort to support Washington's ever hungry army. As if this were not enough, even though the ink was dry on the Treaty of Paris in 1783, these hard times would continue for almost a decade.

Fulfilling the Promise of Independence

In October 1781, New Castle greeted the news of the surrender of the British army at Yorktown with joy, erecting a flagpole for the Congress's Continental colors near the courthouse that were placed "a little above those of the British," which were evidently still flying. Salutes were fired, the town illuminated and toasts drunk. Even more extensive festivities greeted the news of completion of peace negotiations in April 1783.

Despite the festivities, in the long term it seemed that the Revolutionary War had caused economic, political and religious difficulties that would need to be addressed. Three years after the peace was signed, an attempt was made to establish municipal government in New Castle that emphasized the need for order and sobriety because of the "licentiousness which originated from the idleness and relaxation of civil authority" during the Revolutionary War. The effort failed, further postponing the existence of municipal government. The only local government unit recognized by the assembly remained the customary New Castle Hundred. Furthermore, the trustees of New Castle's Common had no means of obtaining revenue from the potentially rich surrounding territory of the Common. Also, slaves and freedmen had tended to join the British, so that Delaware authorities were in no mood to abolish slavery—even gradually. Enlightenment ideas on the need for penal reform and education languished. The assembly had moved Delaware's government from New Castle, making it more sympathetic to the conservative viewpoint of the two southern counties. And then there was the problem of war veterans.

Youthful Peter Jaquett had served in every campaign and battle fought by Haslet's and Hall's Continental regiments, rising from the rank of ensign to major. After seven years of hardship, he returned to New Castle County in 1782 "with scarcely a shirt on his back, or means of getting one, or a shoe on his feet." He was born in 1755, on the family estate of Long Hook, north of New Castle, where the Jaquetts had been for more than a century. Peter was the eldest of eleven children when his father died in 1774. The farm was legally divided between the widow and children, but apparently Peter inherited it or afterward bought much of the estate. His farm, like those of so many war veterans, had gone to ruin during his long absence, and he was so debilitated that with a loan from a friend he took a voyage to the West Indies, which helped him recover his health. Considering that he was a war hero, he became embittered at the problems he faced at home.

After the war ended, Jaquett became poised to discover hidden loyalism. He noted that George Read had in 1783 led in repealing the Loyalist Test Act so that it was no longer an obstacle for loyalists who wished to return to Delaware. Furthermore, he tangled with Read over his right to vote. Read refused to allow him and other war veterans to vote because during their out-of-state service "they had become aliens and that in law and justice had not a right to vote." Read's motives were to keep the electorate as conservative and limited as possible, fearing the republican influence of the war veterans. Ultimately, in a confrontation at the polls, Read did back down. As a result, Jaquett accused Read of being a neo-loyalist and "the greatest curse to this state that heaven ever suffered to live." Here was the beginning of a political rift that would endure.

RELIGIOUS RIVALRY REAPPEARS

Religion should have been the strongest force to bring an end to the breakdown of authority and morality that the war had caused. But at first, it actually contributed to further discord. George Read was again at the center of this controversy, this time as a staunch Anglican. The implications of his influence were portrayed in a book published in 1780 by James Tilton entitled *Timoleon's Biographical History of Dionysius, Tyrant of Delaware*. Another war veteran, Tilton was from a Kent County farm family he left in 1768 to obtain a medical degree from the College of Philadelphia. When the war came, he served ably as surgeon to Haslett's regiment and then as head of military hospitals until 1781. From 1783 to

1785, he was a Delaware delegate to Congress. Tilton found Read to be the tyrant, a man who cultivated religious prejudice for his political ends. He was leading still existing Anglicans against the supposed "violence of republicans and the danger of Presbyterianism." Tilton was not alone in his fears, as he had Jaquett's concerns to build on. They and their allies would perpetuate the Presbyterian alliance that had been formed at the beginning of the Revolution.

Actually, New Castle's meetinghouse had more immediate problems to solve than politics. During most of the war years and until 1791, the meetinghouse was without a pastor, showing the need to attract a minister, regardless of his views. The candidate who finally filled the position was Reverend Samuel Barr, a forty-year-old licentiate of the Londonderry Presbytery in Ulster who had attended the University of Glasgow. He arrived in America in 1784, was immediately ordained by the New Castle Presbytery and was able to preach sporadically at the Christiana Bridge and the New London, Pennsylvania congregations. A year later, he obtained tenure on the frontier in western Pennsylvania at Pittsburgh. He found his meetinghouse dominated by Episcopalians, who resented his efforts to make it strictly Presbyterian. He could not make headway and resigned in 1789, his activities being exonerated by the Presbytery of Virginia. He returned in 1790 to be tested by preaching at New Castle's and Christiana Bridge's meetinghouses for a year before he received a call from the congregations. Described as "a tough little red-haired Ulster-Scot," his debates within the Pittsburg congregation and his background showed him to be an Old Light. It was during Barr's New Castle tenure that several members of the congregation formed the Patriotic Society, a political organization that honored the French Revolution. In 1796, Barr left, and the position was again vacant until 1800.

In that year, John Ewing Latta became pastor of New Castle Presbyterian Church, and because his tenure was long and he had many commitments, there is ample evidence that he was in the Old Light tradition. He favored the influence of the Scottish Presbyterian Church rather than that emanating from the College of New Jersey. He allowed no singing, dancing or shouting in his church. He did hope to use the Bible to unite all Protestants and decried sectarianism. He was open to the rising influence of women and convinced the pious and well-connected Elizabeth Booth to leave her Baptist church. In an 1809 sermon, Latta explained that he was not neutral in politics. He warned of a conspiracy in Europe brought about by the Enlightenment and French Revolution that had now penetrated America and that was formed for "the destruction of all civil order and government, extirpation of every species of morality and

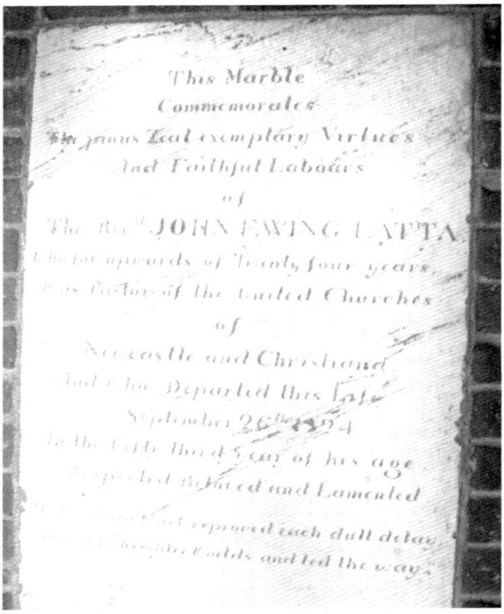

The John Ewing Latta memorial on the New Castle meetinghouse floor commemorates Latta, who became pastor of the church in 1800. He was conservative in that he would allow no singing, dancing or shouting in his church—although not all of his congregation agreed. He was open to the rising influence of women, helping to establish the New Castle Female Bible Society.

religion." This put him firmly in the Federalist political camp, but ample evidence exists to show that some of his congregation did not follow his political or social convictions.

Latta was born in 1771, when the movement for independence was in its infancy. At the age of twenty-nine, he became pastor of the New Castle meetinghouse and also of Christiana Presbyterian Church. He was also one of the first teachers of the New Castle Academy, where he was a master at teaching the classical curriculum. In 1806, he was sent by the Presbytery as a missionary to southern Delaware. He reported that the evangelical Methodists had become dominant there, even though they lacked the "order, decorum and silence" of a Presbyterian religious service. He had a negative view of emotion in religion, within his own church and across town at the Bethany United African Methodist Church, which was described as a hotbed of enthusiasm. Some of his congregation was upset when he banned dancing. Despite his American birth, Latta would continue the traditions of the originating Scottish Church, leading his congregation with skill in the aftermath of the Revolution.

Latta was a sound church administrator and prolific writer. From 1807 until his death, he was clerk of the Presbyterian General Assembly. In 1813, he helped to organize the Bible Society of Delaware and served often as its president. During his tenure, the meetinghouse interior acquired a balcony and was reoriented so that the pulpit was on the south wall, while a rural cemetery was established at the edge of town because of the unsanitary conditions of the church's burial yard. His published sermons include "Christ's Ministers, Watchmen for Souls" (1809); "A Sermon" (1822); and a series from 1812 to 1815 preached on President James Madison's designated days of fasting and thanksgiving during the War of 1812, an activity similar to the Congressional days of fasting that led up to the Revolution. His death came in 1824. Thus, after the war, the two ministers of New Castle's meetinghouse were Old Light rather than New, showing that the ministers continued to be traditional even if their congregation was divided.

Neighboring Immanuel Church emerged from the Revolution with its doors still open, although it was far from being a hub for George Read's political aspirations. A series of meetings and conventions severed the parish's ties to loyalism and established a Delaware Diocese in 1786 and, three years later, a Protestant Episcopal Church of the United States. Representing Immanuel in this movement was Robert Clay, a layman who would be ordained its rector in 1788. The new church had a government separate from that in the mother country, and the *Book of Common Prayer* was revised to be compatible with the values of the new nation.

In New Castle itself, Immanuel's building had deteriorated so much by 1802 that pastor Clay felt that it would become "inconvenient as well as dangerous, for the inhabitants to assemble for public worship." Ten years later, Clay was the only practicing priest in the entire diocese, and he would keep his parish from disintegrating, despite its lack of funds to repair the building. Finally, in 1820, the vestry approved a plan not just for repairs but for the rebuilding and expansion of the sanctuary as well. The effort faltered when it was half completed, but it was rescued by the church's leading families: three Reads, two Booths, two Rogerses and two Janviers. When finished in 1822, the cruciform structure had a tower, two transepts and an impressive

Exaggerated caricature of *Black Methodists Holding a Prayer Meeting*, Philadelphia, by Pavel Petrovich Svinin after John Kimmel, circa 1813. Reverend John Latta and architect Benjamin Latrobe condemned the emotion found in New Castle's black congregations, but their attitude also reflected their hostility to evangelism in any form. A Russian diplomat, Svinin came to the United States as the secretary to the Russian consul-general in Philadelphia, where he traveled and collected views of American life. He bought at least fourteen watercolors from Kimmel, including this one, but in Russia he claimed that it was his work. *Pavel Svinin,* Opyt zhyvopisnavo puteshestviya po severnoi Amerike *(1815).*

Cotemporary view of Immanuel's uplifting steeple, completed in 1822. The burial yard includes the burial stones of George Read Sr. and Gunning Bedford Sr., prominent leaders of New Castle's conservative Independence movement.

steeple that dominated the New Castle skyline. Immanuel finally seemed to have recovered from the Revolutionary War.

Politics aside, it should not be assumed that the Presbyterian and Anglican churches continued to exclusively be foremost in New Castle's religious life. New Protestant denominations of a more evangelical stamp appeared when Baptists and Methodists erected buildings. Bethel Baptist Church had its beginnings in 1786 as a mission of the Welsh Tract Baptist Church in Pencader Hundred. But the log church built two years later was three miles out of town, really serving New Castle Hundred.

In 1773, the Methodist evangelist John Asbury had preached to a large gathering on the Green. While this could be seen as adding religious fervor to the Independence movement, it was nothing of the sort. During the war, Asbury would be forced to hide from the rebels in Kent County, as he staunchly maintained his British citizenship and was a magnet for loyalists. Methodism grew in New Castle only in the early nineteenth century in the form of African American churches, while white Methodists came late to New Castle. A Methodist minister from Wilmington began to preach in New Castle in 1819, and in the next year, land was purchased at the end of the existing Delaware Street for a building. The project went ahead slowly. Thirty years later, a Methodist minister explained the weakness of his New Castle congregation, citing three reasons: "The Episcopal and Presbyterian churches were so much older and their antiquity gives them strength; that there was a greater amount of aristocracy in New Castle than in any other town on the [Delmarva] Peninsula and that our church is not so well suited to aristocracy as others," and that the church was located too far from the center of town.

Separately, St. Peters Roman Catholic Church appeared in the early 1800s as monthly itinerant priests stopped to preach in New Castle. By 1803, the parish had purchased land for a church on Harmony Street, but five years later, it was still unfinished. With the permission of the legislature, a lottery was held to raise funds to complete the church. The lay leadership of St. Peters reflected a change in the immigrant population of New Castle, for Irish Catholics from southern Ireland were now more numerous than the Scots-Irish.

New Castle's Protestant churches were involved in the social reforms by the 1820s. The Bible Society of Delaware was formed in 1813, and its leaders included New Castle's James Booth and Reverend John Latta. While it had been slow to organize, "The Society was intended to embrace persons of every Christian Denomination and therefore the Bible distributed by them shall be without notes." The movement supported a Christian union, not favoring any denomination and aimed to speed the Second Coming of Christ. Latta was the society's first president. He felt that by translating the Bible into the world's various languages and making it accessible, Protestant views could dominate the world. Distribution of the Bible could also heal social and class divisions. Like most reform movements at this time, he emphasized that poor families were to be sought out and assisted by those not only of the middle class but by the rich as well.

It was followed by the New Castle Female Bible Society, established in 1822, with leaders including Ann and Elizabeth Booth, mother and daughter, and Reverend John Latta. They aimed to work outside their households to reach out to economic and ethnic minorities. Of the members, 85 percent were in the top tax-paying brackets, and they did not want women to step out of their proper domestic sphere. They developed social codes of Christian respectability. It was their connection with the broader national Bible movement that sustained them rather than the actual local need for Bibles, a goal that they soon accomplished in New Castle. The women's group raised money and sent it to the parent Delaware Bible Society. Through organizations like this, New Castle's women played a role in stabilizing the society that had been torn by the Revolution.

New Castle's Economy Slowly Revives

One of the great problems of the independence cause was that Continental currency became almost worthless. That is why New Castle businessmen like

Zachariah Van Leuvenigh had refused to take it, even though he knew he would be charged with subverting Congress. Congress finally realized the damage that the currency caused and stopped issuing paper money in 1779. It remained in circulation, however, because debtors favored it, hoping to pay off their obligations in the depreciated currency. The currency also caused hyperinflation in prices, just at the time when foodstuffs became scarce. At the end of 1781, the Delaware Assembly passed an act that refused to recognize Continental or other state currencies as legal tender—something that had been considered treasonable during the early part of the war. This act was the beginning of financial stability that would rebuild New Castle and other Delaware communities.

As noted, New Castle's trade had suffered in the Delaware Valley during and after the Revolution. When trade improved in the 1790s, what was restored was still essentially a coastal trade with Philadelphia. In 1795, four small sloops constantly sailed between New Castle and Philadelphia, and a decade later, seven larger packets had replaced them. It was in New Castle that Philadelphia ships again took on vegetables and poultry, with their captains joining them by land after settling accounts in Philadelphia. Beyond provisions, New Castle was a market for lumber and firewood, oak selling for five dollars per cord and hickory for nearly seven. By 1816, the new municipal government was asked to regulate the sale of two commodities, lumber and hay.

Previous page, above and below: *A View of the Town of New Castle from the River Delaware*, by Ives le Blanc, July 4, 1797. It shows large wharfs jutting into the river. Thomas Bond's store advertises that flaxseed was wanted, a cargo that would fetch a good price in Ireland's linen industry. *Courtesy the Hargraves family and James Meek.*

A view of the port of New Castle was painted by Ives Blanc in 1797, the year New Castle finally achieved municipal government. The painting and the Latrobe map of 1805 show five large wharfs jutting into the river. They belonged to Archibald Alexander, who constructed an alley leading directly to his wharf; James Riddle and John Bird, rich and politically involved merchants; John Janvier, of that ancient New Castle family; and Thomas Bond, who had his store and the Stage Tavern at his wharf's Front Street entrance. The fifth and longest wharf, owned by James McCullough, was docking for the regular packet boats, and it was the home of the ferry that plied to New Jersey. Because silting prevented the ferry from landing at low tide, this wharf was farther extended into the river.

New Castle's further claim to fame as a port was as a pivotal point on the route to Baltimore on Chesapeake Bay. Goods and passengers that took the packets from Philadelphia were unloaded at New Castle and then conveyed by stage, carts and heavy wagons to Frenchtown on the Elk River, which emptied into Chesapeake Bay. This route had been evident in 1775 when New Castle's Joseph Tatlow owned and operated the transportation from Philadelphia to Frenchtown, while someone else controlled the navigation on the Chesapeake. Revival of the route after the war gave New Castle's economy a boost.

While this last route was impassible in the winter, the port of New Castle functioned longer in the winter than either Philadelphia or Wilmington. The five-mile width of the river at New Castle helped to make the harbor as ice-free as possible for ships to winter over. The Delaware legislature authorized a lottery in 1794 from which $12,000 was raised to build four masonry piers to beak up the ice. While over the years the piers required considerable repair, they helped to allow shipping to continue in the winter season. An 1802 law authorized the appointment of a harbor master, evidently based on current or future need. Three years later, Congress was petitioned to have New Castle made a port of entry, but the effort was turned down, although the rebuilt masonry piers were placed under federal control to maintain them.

While local and coastal trade was the main thrust, New Castle's port was not without Atlantic trade. When James Booth applied in 1789 for the position of the state's first federal customs collector, he noted that Irish ports still brought indentured servants to New Castle and that a few vessels came from the West Indies. Some stopped at New Castle before they reached Philadelphia so that they could send their passengers or cargo overland to

Frenchtown and then to Baltimore and Virginia. Thomas Bond's wharf store advertised that he wanted to purchase flaxseed to sell in the Irish market, an ideal cargo for the return voyage to Ireland. American merchants also benefited from European wars, which caused food shortages that their neutral ships could remedy.

The port was flourishing enough to attract the Aull family in 1794, led by sea captain William and his brother, John, from Londonderry, Ulster. Behind their double-door Front Street houses, one wood frame and the other of brick, was their own spacious dock on the river. Captain William gave an engraved 1793 Scottish Bible to the Presbyterian church, and in 1800, he and John purchased a pew. Two years before, William had been elected one of the town's first Five Commissioners. John repaired ships and not only built his house on Front Street but also erected wood-frame row and double houses on Second Street. After William's untimely death in

William Aull House, circa 1798. William had this double-door house built of brick. With marble key plates above the windows, the Federal-style house was occupied by this Ulster sea captain only briefly.

John Aull House, circa 1790. William's brother, John, a master carpenter who repaired ships, built this originally double-door house, inheriting and living in both houses after William's death. The boards covering the older wood-frame house purposely do not overlap but rather are meant to look as if the surface was of smooth stone.

the early 1800s, John inherited his estate and used both houses. Like other neighboring wharf owners, John's politics were those of a Democratic-Republican. He died in New Castle in 1828.

AGRICULTURAL IMPROVEMENT

In 1804, the New Castle County Agricultural Association was formed to raise "a spirit of rational inquiry" into farming. Well-educated Dr. George Munro, John Bird (a "Jeffersonian merchant") and the merchant and wharf owner James Riddle were active members. Such gentlemen followed the model of English gentry, believing in the ideal of virtue in the cultivation of land. In fact, those who shared the ideals of the Enlightenment would support President Thomas Jefferson's view that agriculture was the true source of wealth.

The members may also have read Robert Livingston's *Essay on Sheep* from 1810, which was available from the New Castle Library Company. It inspired the breeding and cultivation of sheep, which were driven to market at either New Castle or Philadelphia. From 1780 to 1827, the number of

Sheep from Robert Livingston's *Essay on Sheep*, 1810. The text was available from the New Castle Library Company, inspiring the breeding and cultivation of sheep, which were driven to market at either New Castle or Philadelphia. From 1780 to 1827, the number of sheep in New Castle Hundred increased, although most farmers had small herds. *Courtesy New Castle Historical Society.*

sheep in New Castle Hundred would increase, although most farmers had small herds, the largest numbering ninety-four. Here was a new means of diversifying agriculture.

Leasing the Common

Despite the creation of the trustees in 1764, for the next twenty-five years, covering the entire Revolutionary War, it is assumed that they met but did very little business. The trustees complained that the Common remained uncultivated and that the inhabitants did not derive "any considerable advantages from it." Since the land around it was productively cultivated, the Common must have been a great contrast to its neighbors. Had it continued in the traditional English manner, the trustees could not have developed income from rents, which ultimately could be used to create public improvements and cover taxes in New Castle. It would take another act to expand the trustees' powers so that a portion of the Common could be leased to other parties.

On November 3, 1789, as Delaware was involved the effort to put the first United States Constitution into effect, the trustees approached the Penn family's agent, Edmund Physick, to expand their powers and permit them to rent out the land. Starting in 1791, minutes of the trustee meetings show that again the Penns agreed to the trustees' request. As of November 19, 1791, they approved the rental and productive use of Common land, allowing for growth in the income of the trustees. While the land could still not be sold, leasing was a popular alternative.

CONTROVERSY WITH THE STATE OF DELAWARE

Delaware politics, however, intervened from the new capital, Dover, where interests were rarely favorable to New Castle. The legal-minded trustees had completed the agreement in 1791 with the Penns that accepted the precedent that they owned the Common, regardless of the independence of the United States. Thomas McKean had been hired by the proprietors to act with their agent to settle questions of rent and ownership in all the Penns' Delaware lands. They offered the governor of Delaware as head of the state the first rights to purchase such lands. But this was not how the assembly viewed it, for it felt that the trustees' request had ignored the sovereignty of the state. The assembly claimed that the Penns had never held title to Delaware lands, that McKean and the Penns had no hold over them and that it was a criminal act to accept vacant land from anyone except the state. Later, the assembly would abrasively confiscate all the Penns' lands without offering the family any compensation as had been done by Pennsylvania's government.

In reaction to the high-handed Delaware Assembly in 1793, Thomas McKean published *A Calm Appeal to the People of Delaware*, which claimed that many people would prefer to deal with the Penns rather than with the State of Delaware in the leasing and selling of the Penn properties. It hinted that a new election was necessary to clean the house of the assembly in Dover. McKean, who was now chief justice of Pennsylvania's Supreme Court, claimed that the Delaware Assembly's actions violated the Peace of Paris and the Delaware and federal Constitutions. The Delaware Assembly was not about to take criticism from the former New Castle resident and Trustees of the Common, and their legislation stood. McKean's effort was meant to help the trustees, but he also alienated the assembly. What had begun as a simple effort to expand the trustees' powers ended up as a legal duel over state's rights, as McKean accused the state of Delaware of using powers that belonged to the new federal government.

The Common Leases

Sentiments for agricultural improvement appeared among the Trustees of the Common when George Munro and Archibald Alexander helped draft the first rent requirements for the Common lands. They were out to force improvement, thus they compelled the tenants to invest in hedging and ditching their fields. The annual rent was due at the end of the first rental year. However, most potential tenants could not meet such rigid demands, and the requirements had to be modified. The annual rent obligation was eased in February 1794 to require it at the end of the fourth year. Two years later, leases were no longer heavy with improvement stipulations but were offered simply "upon the best terms that can be agreed upon."

Painting by Vernon Good of a farmhouse, lease no. 6, or the Penn Farm in the Common, 1950s. *Courtesy Trustees of the Common.*

By the early 1800s, the Common was divided into tenant farms, with a small portion still being reserved for New Castle's inhabitants. The farms were numbered: no. 1 became the Jefferson Farm, nos. 2 and 4 became the Stockton Farm, no. 3 became the Oglethorpe Farm, no. 5 became known as Centre Hall, nos. 6 and 7 became the Penn Farm and no. 8 became the Union Farm. The first tenant of 1797 was John Hair, who ran a tavern at "Hare's Corners" that was a meeting place for cattle drovers on their way to Philadelphia.

Trustee Dr. George Monro deserves further explanation because he was the most enlightened leader in New Castle County. His Scottish father had moved to New Castle, where George was born in 1760. As a young man, he gained a medical degree from the College of Philadelphia, and during the war, he served as medical officer to the Virginia Line. The high point of his education came after the war in 1783, when he went to the British Isles, studying medicine in London and taking another degree from the University of Edinburg, one the great centers of the Scottish Enlightenment. Upon his return in 1786, he married Jemma Haslet, the daughter of Colonel John, and they settled on a farm in St. George's Hundred and, later, on one in Christiana. In the next decades, until his death in 1819, Monro was involved in reform causes that many Delaware politicians avoided. Like most of the Founding Fathers, he became a deist, although late in life he turned Presbyterian. He supported Delaware's constitution of 1792 and was elected to the House under its broad franchise. He was active in an effort to found a college at Wilmington and finance secondary schools, unpopular causes because they involved raising taxes. His presence on a committee ensured that the Enlightenment was alive in New Castle County.

INCOME FROM THE COMMON

The first major trustee appropriation from the rental proceeds came in 1801 for the building of a school on a portion of the Green that a year later was named the New Castle Academy. The building had been erected two years before on the basis of private subscription, following a design of Philadelphia master builder Peter Crowding. In 1802, it was chartered to provide the first classical education for New Castle's sons, with many of its trustees being drawn from the Trustees of the Common. The Academy charged tuition,

The Academy, 1799. It was built ultimately with funds from the Trustees of the Common, according to the design of Philadelphia master builder Peter Crowding. In 1802, it was chartered to provide the first classical education for New Castle's sons, with many of its trustees being drawn from the Trustees of the Common. The Academy charged tuition, serving as private school for the elite.

Portrait of Benjamin Henry Latrobe, circa 1804, by Charles Willson Peale. In 1804, the Trustees of the Common hired Benjamin Latrobe, President Jefferson's surveyor of public buildings, to do a survey of New Castle. Completed the next year, it became the basis for trustee improvements of the roads and infrastructure. *From* Impressions Respecting New Orleans: Diary & Sketches, 1818–1820.

serving as private school for the elite. It never became a college, and New Castle still lacked public schools.

Other trustee projects appeared as result of an 1805 survey completed by none other than President Jefferson's surveyor of public buildings, Benjamin Latrobe, which caused sidewalks to be placed and streets to be extended and graded, although not paved. By 1807, the trustees had purchased streetlights for the town. Fifteen years later, the trustees bought the town clock and installed it in the Immanuel Church steeple; they continued to pay for the clock into the twentieth century. To support New Castle's port, the trustees reconstructed the wharf at the foot of Harmony Street. From 1823 on, the trustees developed the town's first water system by boring artesian wells. The Trustees of the Common funded the improvements; thus, the public benefited and did not have to pay.

TRUSTEE LEADERSHIP

The trustees involved in the controversy with the state overextending its powers in 1791 were George Read Sr. (chair), David Finney, Gunning Bedford, John Stockton, Kensey Johns, Joseph Tatlow, James Booth Sr., George Read Jr., James Riddle, Archibald Alexander, Joseph Boggs, Matthew Pearce and John Silsbee. Both Reads, father and son, were now present and thus the leading family. George Read Jr. lived in James Booth's house while his own home was being built in the early 1800s. The elder Read had taught Kensey Johns to be an attorney, and he was now a member of the assembly. Another Read protégé was Gunning Bedford, who married George Read's sister, Mary, and attended the family's Immanuel Church. Bedford's political career would take off after the war when he was elected to the assembly and the Legislative Council. Those without a close connection to the Reads were merchants, wharf owners James Riddle and Archibald Alexander, as well as Joseph Tatlow, who had monopolized the trade route from Philadelphia to Chesapeake Bay by way of New Castle.

AVOIDING THE EVIL OF SLAVERY

Earlier, John Dickinson's *Letters From a Pennsylvania Farmer* had claimed that "we are taxed without our own consent…we are therefore slaves." The rhetoric of the Revolution saw slavery only in terms of rights of whites; blacks were ignored. Revolutionary War leaders like Dickinson, Thomas McKean, George Read, David Finney, Kensey Johns and Gunning Bedford Sr. were all slaveholders. The federal Constitution of 1787 also failed to address the issue of slavery, except in terms of proportional representation, where slaves would be counted as two-thirds of a white male. Thus, the record during and immediately after the Revolutionary War showed little effort on the part of the Founding Fathers to address a long-existing controversy.

Finally in 1787, the Delaware Assembly took the initiative and began to remove the obstacles to manumission and the rights of freedmen that had been created in the mid-eighteenth century. The assembly forbade the exportation of free blacks from Delaware, and slaves imported into Delaware were granted their freedom, while the importer was fined. Free blacks had the right to hold property and initiate court proceedings to defend it. However, they were denied the right to vote and could not hold public office or give evidence in a court against whites. To further manumission, slave owners no longer had to post bond for slaves they freed. The prevention of the slave trade and the easing of restrictions on freedmen still left slavery intact, although the principle of individual manumission was accepted.

New Castle was less supportive of the abolitionist movement than Wilmington or Dover, probably because it lacked a strong Quaker element in its population. When the Delaware Society for Promoting the Abolition of Slavery was formed in 1788, recognizing that manumission was a halfway measure, only George Munro of New Castle's leaders would become a member. The society proved to be too much ahead of its time as far as the legislature was concerned, for slavery would not be abolished in Delaware until federal amendments at the end of the Civil War intervened.

Even when free, New Castle's blacks were treated as inherently dangerous. In 1809, a petition complained that activities like the "trading, dealing and bartering of servants and slaves without the consent of their owner" was "an evil practice to the great injury of many of the inhabitants of the town… and neighborhood." It was not only their petty capitalism that bothered the petitioners but also their disorderly assembly without supposedly lawful business, "to the great disturbance of the peaceable inhabitants." Furthermore, as they now had no masters, they needed to be regulated by the state. This was especially true when they inundated the market, which was an important source of their food. The legislature developed codes that prevented blacks from voting, buying or selling alcohol, carrying guns and traveling without passes signed by whites.

Despite these prohibitions, African Americans in New Castle grew to be numerous enough to gather and build their own houses of worship. In 1806, on stopover in New Castle because of the Sabbath, Benjamin Latrobe looked up a black Methodist preacher he had known during his New Castle surveying and, with a black sailor and his captain, attended a

Bethany United African Methodist Church, 1868. With the guidance of Peter Spencer of Wilmington, blacks developed a congregation that in 1817 was incorporated as Bethany UAM Church. In the next year, a wood-frame church was constructed at Fourth and Williams Streets. The congregation bought the adjoining lot and constructed this larger masonry building, which was completed in 1868. It was the first black congregation in New Castle, although others soon followed.

black Methodist service. New Castle's blacks had been influenced by the formation of a church in Philadelphia in 1793 that practiced Methodism, although it had been created as a protest against the segregation found in the Methodist Church. Peter Spencer of Wilmington appeared and was instrumental in establishing this New Castle church. On October 27, 1817, blacks incorporated the Bethany United African Methodist Church. During the next year, a wood-frame church about sixty feet square was constructed at Fourth and Williams Street. The governing bodies of the church were made up completely of African Americans. Other black churches would follow. On their own rather than through the antislavery movement, blacks became a part of the New Castle community.

Support for the Federal Constitution, Not the Federalist Party

A Federal Convention met in Philadelphia from May 1787 to draft a new constitution, which was needed because the Articles of Confederation that had carried Congress through the war represented a states' rights rather than federal government. For the next five months, the delegates would debate and hammer out compromises to create a stronger federal government. Again active, New Castle's George Read was among them, along with his friend John Dickinson of Kent County. Read was an extreme Federalist; he found state government useless and proposed that senators hold office for life.

The greatest of the convention's compromises directly affected Delaware. As representatives of a small state, the Delaware delegation supported the concept of equal vote in representation rather than a proportional vote in which the small states would be overwhelmed by those with large populations. Delaware already had a history of being dominated by its larger neighbors, Pennsylvania and Maryland, and in June 1776, the assembly had made a point of severing its longstanding ties to the government of Pennsylvania. Its support of an equal vote for each state continued the practice that Congress had operated under during the Revolution, each state delegation of whatever size being asked to develop a consensus so as to cast one vote. The larger states noted how undemocratic this was in a republic, where it was necessary to represent the diverse views of a segmented population. The smaller states were unmoved by such arguments and pointed out that the larger states were divided on the details of how bring about the radical idea of proportional representation. The key moment came when a bicameral legislature was proposed, with equal representation for states in the Senate and proportional representation for states in the House of Representatives. Here the concept of a balance of powers prevailed. While Delaware was not enthusiastic about the compromise, it did accept it.

As a small state with a majority of conservatives, Delaware could move quickly to approve the Federal Convention's Constitution. Before 1787 was up, on December 7 the Delaware Convention met and "approved, assented to, ratified, and confirmed" the federal Constitution drafted in Philadelphia. James Latimer of nearby Newport presided over the convention and led the New Castle County delegation. Signatories from New Castle included Gunning Bedford Sr., Kensey Johns and John James. George Read was not elected to the convention.

Writing more than a decade after the event, Presbyterian minister John Mason lamented that the "Federal Constitution makes no acknowledgement of that God who gave us our national existence." Mindful of citizenship, he declared that the founders had forgotten Christianity. Actually, the Constitution established the principle that the care of souls was not the business of government, leading to the concept of separation between church and state.

The Delaware Constitution of 1776 had always been a halfway measure of unfulfilled promises, and the federal Constitution made it look especially outmoded. Finally, in 1792, a new Delaware Constitution was written at a convention held in Dover by delegates that included New Castle County's Kensey Johns and George Monro. Like the federal Constitution, it proposed a balance of three branches of government. The chief executive was strengthened with the authority to appoint officers, and the title was changed from "president" to "governor." The legislature became bicameral, and the Privy Council disappeared. Property qualifications for white males to vote were ended, thus expanding the voter base and the influence of political parties. The judiciary was established separately and the number of judges cut, while the courts were reorganized. A bill of rights was added to this constitution, ensuring the fundamental protection of citizens. Following the trend of the federal Constitution, no clergyman or preacher of any denomination was allowed to hold a civil office in Delaware, or be a member of either branch of the legislature, as long as the clergyman exercised a pastoral or clerical function.

Revolution in Town Government

The real revolution in New Castle was the establishment of town government. New Castle had tried unsuccessfully to obtain a permanent charter as a town from the three counties or state legislature in 1672, 1724 and after the Revolution in 1786. The 1724 draft charter had included the positions of mayor and clerk of the market, but it was in effect for only a year. Consistently, the Delaware legislature was interested in strong counties, not expanding cities or towns. Even when town government was established with the Five Commissioners, they would be still dependent on acts of the legislature to alter their powers. When the commissioners wanted to remove swine so as to keep them from roaming the streets, they had to appeal to the Delaware legislature for approval.

In 1796, informal town meetings were held from which another request originated for a state law that authorized the creation of town government through the election of Five Commissioners. While this was not a charter, in the next year it was approved by the legislature, which named the first Five Commissioners: Archibald Alexander, James Booth, John Crow, George Read Jr. and Nicholas Van Dyke. Alexander was chair. They were given the power to set boundaries for the town. In the first election in May 1798, the taxable residents of the town returned three of the serving commissioners but replaced Booth and Read with John Bird and William Aull. At one time or another, all these commissioners would also serve as Trustees of the Common, and many would be Presbyterians.

After town government was established, in the early 1800s a segment of New Castle's population held town meetings to discuss increasing the powers of the Five Commissioners. Others, however, distrusted formal government and feared what they felt was the tyranny of a majority of the voters. The effort to delegate authority to elected officials and hired professionals gradually gained momentum—Latrobe's contracted survey is the earliest example. However, from then until 1826, when the government moved into the Town Hall, it had no home. It was not regarded as a high priority because town taxes were levied inconsistently, only when there was a demonstrated need for money, and the Trustees of the Common covered the expenses of capital improvements. New Castle was not yet a strong municipality.

The Five Commissioners gradually took over the duties that had been previously performed by the Market Trustees. In the 1797 town law, the commissioners were given the power to create the elected position of clerk of the market. The clerk was charged with collecting stall rents set by the commissioners, ranging from two cents per day to four dollars per year. He also inspected the building for cleanliness, maintained the accuracy of the weights and measures and upheld law and order in the market. In 1810, it was suggested that pigs running at large should be caught by the clerk, who would sell them for damages. The commissioners also created two similar positions, wood corder and flour inspector, reflecting the importance of these two commodities. Market regulation was now the duty of the new town government.

Many of the Trustees of the Common were among the Five Commissioners designated to govern the town. In the future, two-thirds of the trustees would serve as commissioners, and over half held these positions simultaneously. Thus, the funds of the trustees and the chartered authority of the commissioners would be in the same hands.

POLITICAL PARTIES

With the war ended, New Castle's Nicholas Van Dyke was president of Delaware, and when his daughter married, George Washington was the most honored guest. Like Washington, Van Dyke was at first a man who stood above political faction and tried to be aloof from all political persuasions. A wealthy planter, Van Dyke did not have to have a party affiliation to be elected one of the original town commissioners. His early political aloofness would not last, as he become a Federalist to be elected to represent Delaware in 1808 at the United States House of Representatives and in 1817 at the Senate.

In the approval of the new federal Constitution, rudimentary political parties made their appearances, as distinct groups were for or against the new Constitution. These emerging parties were not yet the disciplined, spoils-oriented organizations that would evolve by the 1830s. This meant that Thomas McKean or John Dickinson could easily switch his allegiance to run on a particular ticket. Moreover, parties did not exist within New Castle's government, for the town elections were nonpartisan, the smallest unit of party organization being the hundred.

When political parties appeared in the 1790s, Delaware accepted the Federalist solution more than other states. The Federalists had made Delaware the first state to ratify the new federal Constitution in 1787 and, remarkably, remained in power until the 1820s, longer than in any other state. They supported a constitution that would provide extensive powers for a central government to promote law and order. They attracted landlords, attorneys

Rear view of the Nicholas Van Dyke House, 1930s, erected in 1738. It was an early Georgian-style house that from the back was not nearly as large as its imposing façade conveys. It was built for Dr. John Finney, and at his death, it was leased by Van Dyke from 1774 to 1785. He was a member of the independence-oriented New Castle County Committee, representative to Congress and one of the early presidents of Delaware, 1783–86. *Courtesy New Castle Historical Society.*

and merchants, who sought political deference, dominance over land through credit and a strong military to control crowds and debtors. They felt that much could still be learned from the British Constitution and copied its intuitions like a national bank and valued its merchants as trading partners. Thus, they were liable to be attacked as neo-loyalists. George Washington and Alexander Hamilton were their mentors. At this time, Federalists like George Read Sr., Gunning Bedford Sr., Kensey Johns, Nicholas Van Dyke and James Booth dominated the Trustees of the Common, although other political persuasions could be found within its membership.

New Castle's Democratic-Republicans

Despite their ascendancy in the rest of Delaware, the one place in the state that the Federalists did not rule was New Castle. There the opposition Democratic-Republicans held a majority. They followed Thomas Jefferson, idealizing the yeoman farmer, the virtue of outright ownership of his land

and sympathy for the ordinary farmer that prevented foreclosure for debt. They felt that the powers of the states needed to be defended against the encroaching federal government. This emerging party attracted members who sought minimal government expenditures, low taxes, credit relief, emissions of paper money, conventions of people and crowd action out-of-doors. In foreign affairs, France, the United States' most prominent Revolutionary War ally, was the nation to be emulated. Thus, New Castle was again politically out of step with the rest of Delaware.

In New Castle, from 1794 on, Democratic-Republicans received a warm welcome at the Patriotic Society of New Castle County, which favored the demise of the French Old Regime in a revolution that used the guillotine. They were familiar with the ideas of Peter Jaquett and James Tilton that had identified George Read Sr. as the arch-Federalist. The merchants who owned New Castle's wharfs led the society. Its presidents included James McCullough, innkeeper, and Archibald Alexander, town commissioner. Alexander and James Riddle would be unsuccessful Democratic-Republican candidates for governor. The secretary was Commissioner John Bird, who would be elected senator in 1800. Another member, Nicholas Van Dyke Jr., was exceptional in that he was considered a moderate Federalist like his father. All but Bird were at this time Presbyterians. Since merchants were usually Federalists, the merchant leadership of the Democratic-Republicans was again out of character with the rest of Delaware.

The Federalists attacked McCullough and Alexander as leaders of an illegal organization. The election for governor in 1795 was a contest between New Castle's leaders, Gunning Bedford Sr. (Episcopalian/Presbyterian) and Alexander (Presbyterian). Bedford won narrowly by carrying Kent and Sussex Counties, while New Castle County went for Alexander. To provide Alexander with balm for his defeat, two years later, McCullough held a dinner at his inn in honor of Bastille Day.

Dr. Archibald Alexander was now as influential in New Castle as George Read Sr. Born in 1756 in Staunton, Virginia, Alexander was from a family that had emigrated from Donegal, Ulster, to Maryland in the late seventeenth century. In the Revolutionary War, he first served in the Virginia militia but then joined the Tenth Virginia Continental Regiment as surgeon. After two years as a Continental, he left to serve on a privateer based in Norfolk, Virginia. Caught up in the civil conflict, his ship was taken by the Royal Navy, and he became a prisoner on a ship in New York Harbor, where he languished for most of the war.

Archibald Alexander House, circa 1800. An imposing residence in the Federal/Georgian style with decorative keystones above some of the windows. Born in 1752 in Virginia, Alexander was the first chairman of the town's Five Commissioners, a trustee of the Presbyterian church and the academy and a wharf owner. He was New Castle's leading Democratic-Republican, one of the two political parties spawned in 1787 in the debate over passage of the federal Constitution.

Alexander came to New Castle in the early 1780s, where he was a doctor, surgeon and politician. In 1785, he settled down, marrying Mary Enos. He became a Trustee of the Common in 1791, showing that the trustees were not exclusively Federalists. Alexander also became chairman of the Five Commissioners and a trustee of the Presbyterian Church and the Academy. From 1791 to 1798, he was three times a state senator and once a state representative. He also served in 1801 as chief clerk of the New Castle County Court of Common Pleas. Later, along with Dr. George Monro, he supported the establishment of a fund for secondary schools.

The Democratic-Republicans did have success on the national level. Their leader, Thomas Jefferson, was elected president in 1800 over the Federalist candidate, John Adams. Jefferson commented that his election was "as real a revolution in the principles of our government as that of 1776 was in its form." Jefferson used the term "revolution" not as a radical creation of a new order but rather in the sense of a return to first principles, of a restoration of original values and ideals that had been overturned or repudiated. For him, the election of 1800 was a revolution because it marked a turning back to the true republican spirit of 1776. In his eyes, a minority faction of Federalists had captured control of that government immediately after the passage of the Constitution of 1787. Now he wanted to implement the principles of a republican revolution. Jefferson's fundamental goal in 1801 was to end what he felt was the threatened "Anglicization" of American government and society. The Democratic-Republicans would be entrenched in the White House for the next twenty-five years. In the Jeffersonian sense, the revolution came back to New Castle.

NEW CASTLE'S PRESBYTERIAN GOVERNOR

In the late eighteenth century, Charles and Susanna McCallmont Thomas lived south of New Castle on Dragon Neck in Red Lion Hundred, New Castle County. They moved to New Castle, where he became an elder in the Presbyterian meetinghouse and president of the New Castle Turnpike Company. He was a Democratic-Republican, a colleague of Archibald Alexander and James McCullough. In 1801, to take advantage of travelers using his turnpike, he contracted with Philadelphia builder Peter Crowding to erect a hotel at the corner of Front and Harmony Streets that would also serve as the family compound. The structure had a narrow front, but it expanded on the Harmony Street side to make it one of the town's largest buildings.

Charles Thomas Jr. was born in New Castle in 1790 and grew up there. He married Eliza Stoops, and they had one child, Eliza, while they lived in the family compound. Charles and Eliza were members of New Castle Presbyterian Church. However, their daughter had to be cared for by Dr. John Rumsey of Wilmington until she was about ten years old, and then she moved in with Charles's sister, Sally, who was married to William Read, the son of George Read Jr. Charles had befriended the Read family when he attended Princeton College, where his roommate was William. Charles studied law with his father, who was compatibly a Democratic-Republican. William and Sally also resided at the Thomas House hotel and eventually owned it.

Charles was admitted to the Delaware Bar in 1813 and began to practice law in New Castle. He chose his father's Democratic-Republican Party when he commenced his state political career. He was elected in 1818 to the House

Thomas House. Charles Thomas Sr. had the hotel-residence built in 1801. Charles Thomas Jr. lived there and was one of the few Democratic-Republicans to hold the office of governor, presiding for about seven months, 1823–24. After his frustrating service as governor, he retired from politics altogether, spending the rest of his life in New Castle.

and in 1822 and 1823 to the Senate. James Monroe's national administration was in power, the last Democratic-Republican and Virginia dynasty president and a president Charles supported. Since he was the Speaker of the Delaware Assembly in the 1823 session, Charles succeeded to the governorship when two-time and Democratic-Republican governor Joseph Haslet died in office. As the Federalists dominated the state, Democratic-Republications had rarely been able to capture Delaware's governorship. Democratic-Republican governor David Hall had broken the monopoly in 1802, but the majority of governors were still Federalists. Thus, Charles Thomas "came through the back door" as the youngest man ever to hold the office and a rare Democratic-Republican. He presided from June 24, 1823, to January 20, 1824. After his frustrating experience as governor, he retired from politics altogether. He spent the rest of his life in New Castle and was buried at the Presbyterian rural cemetery upon his death in 1848.

While governor, Charles Thomas continued the Democratic-Republican advocacy for improvement of public education, a cause that George Munro and Archibald Alexander had introduced. Taxes for education were always unpopular, but Thomas supported a special school tax that he promised would relieve people of the most intolerable of all burdens, immorality and ignorance. He asserted that the elective franchise and civil rights were useless if citizens were unable to read the tickets presented at the polls: "Such men may think themselves free, but in fact they are slaves...If education is confined to the rich." Again, however, the assembly refused to raise taxes for local education.

Thomas was also an advocate for penal reform. New Castle County's courthouse and jail seemed to be immune to the ideas of the Enlightenment, which asserted that punishment for a crime should reflect the degree of violence to society and that the state had a duty to reform a prisoner while in jail so that the person did not remain a criminal. Instead, justice in New Castle seemed to be based on the harshness of colonial punishment on the Green. An engraving of the combination whipping post and stocks still on the Green in 1882 was entitled by reporters from *Frank Leslie's Illustrated Newspaper* as *Relic of Barbarism*. It shows delinquents in the stocks suspended

Relic of Barbarism, 1882. It shows the combination whipping post and stocks still on the Green in 1882. Delinquents are in the stocks suspended above the whipping post, where a hand-shackled black male is being flayed by a cat-o'-nine-tails. The crowd of families with children, both black and white, seems well entertained. The reporters claimed that the punishment was a state policy that was obstinately maintained. *From* Frank Leslie's Illustrated Newspaper, *August 26, 1882.*

above the whipping post, where a hand-shackled black male is being flayed by a cat-o'-nine-tails. The crowd of families with children, both black and white, seems well entertained. The reporters claimed that the punishment was a state policy that was obstinately maintained.

Whether Thomas witnessed such punishment in New Castle is unclear, but he noted critically that "the penal laws of this State are much severer than those of any State in the Union." Arguing against imprisonment for debt, an article of faith of the Federalist creed, he claimed that "[a]n opinion seems to pervade the community that our poor houses...are rather nurseries for vice than asylums for the helpless." His request for penal reform received no response from the Federalist legislature.

After the war, New Castle's early leadership in the Independence movement was absorbed by a viable two-party system, rather than the dominance of a single party. New Castle not only led in the development of Democratic-Republicans, but it also had important Federalists. This was unique in Delaware because elsewhere in the state the Federalists usually held the reins of government.

The Town Hall

When the New Castle Town Hall was built in 1826, the town's economy was again flagging. The construction of the civic building was meant to give the economy a badly needed boost. The Town Hall was underwritten by the Trustees of the Common in cooperation with the town commissioners. In July 1825, most of the trustees who approved the erection of the Town Hall were new, beyond the generation that had survived the Revolution. The only recognizable name is George Read Jr., who had sat with his father, George Sr., among the trustees of 1791. Now he was on his own, although his father never felt that his son matched his potential. For a start, he had joined the Democratic-Republicans, the party that branded his father as a neo-loyalist and persecutor of war veterans. He also failed to equal his father as an attorney and did not hold on to his appointed position as a town commissioner. Instead, he strove to be a socially prominent gentleman by erecting the community's largest and most elegant house. Completed in 1804 by Philadelphia craftsmen, who were rarely paid on time, this monument was so expensive that it put him in debt.

The money for the erection of the Town Hall was borrowed from New Castle's Farmer's Bank of Delaware against the rents that the trustees

Above: Houses of George Read Sr. and Jr., 1805 survey, Benjamin Latrobe and assistants. George Sr.'s modest house stood in what is today the garden of the George Read Jr. House. George Jr. followed in his father's footsteps, but his father never felt that he matched his potential. The son strove to be socially prominent by erecting the community's largest Federal/Georgian-style house, dwarfing his father's house. *Courtesy Delaware Public Archives.*

Below: Contemporary view of Town Hall, 1826. It houses the offices of the Trustees of the Common and the meeting room of the city council.

were to receive from the Common. Such loans had first been necessary in 1801, when the trustees contributed to opening the academy building. The first loan for erecting the Town Hall was in September 1825 for $1,000, and three others followed. All told, the building cost between $6,000 and $7,000. The structure was insured in September 1826 for $3,000. The superintendent for the structure was Peter Delany, sheriff of New Castle County. Chief of Maintenance Thomas Turner was charged with airing, sweeping and cleaning the rooms, as well as attending trustee meetings to make reports. In December 1826, the United States government signed a lease for a room in the Town Hall. This is thought to have given it proximity to legal activities in the Courthouse. At last, the Five Commissioners and the Trustees of the Common had a home.

Affirmations

New Castle's role in the Revolutionary era was far more complicated than it is usually portrayed. It can be roughly divided into four periods: the early years of political opposition to Britain that led to the Declaration of Independence, the invasion and naval occupation of General William Howe, the later war years of civil and naval conflict along the Delaware Estuary and the aftermath of economic revival and political parties in the wake of the new federal and state constitutions.

From 1774 to 1776, New Castle was the center of Delaware's Independence movement. Its Presbyterian meetinghouse, the Green and the Courthouse were scenes of debate that recognized the authority of Congress and the need for a new government. Proximity to Philadelphia, where Congress met, caused New Castle to respond fully to Congress's calls for days of thanksgiving and prayer. Here the militia was rallied and the state's first constitution written.

These conditions changed during the British invasion and presence of 1777–78. New Castle's militia was mustered and served at the Battle of Cooch's Bridge in an effort to stop Howe, who went on to defeat Washington at Brandywine and capture Philadelphia. While not garrisoned by the British, New Castle had the Royal Navy at its doorstep, and many of its farmers and craftsmen supplied its ships. As the beginning of a trend, the Delaware legislature had ordered the coast, including New Castle, abandoned so that the enemy would not benefit from the bounty of its countryside. With the Royal Navy present, the town was emptied of its rebel leadership as they left for their country estates or inland relatives. This allowed the minority of loyalists to flourish as never before. Some gained positions in the Royal Navy, and when the British decided to evacuate Philadelphia, most New Castle loyalists left in the departing British ships.

Logically, with the British forces gone to New York, New Castle's rebels could return and experience a revival of the prosperity experienced before the war. Instead, New Castle suffered, for two reasons. It was no longer the seat of Delaware's government. The lower two counties had always resented New Castle as the colonial capital, and the abandonment of New Castle had ultimately included the state government, which was finally moved to Dover. Secondly, war on the Delaware River continued until peace negotiations in 1783. It was not another British invasion but a civil war between rebels and loyalists, focusing on the coast but spreading inland and involving refugee raiders, privateers and a few Royal Navy or state navy ships. The British blockade prevented vessels in Philadelphia's port from sailing on the river and beyond Delaware Bay. New Castle did have an admiralty court that could judge and sell prizes taken by the rebels. This was the civil war that had been so feared by the Presbyterian Synod in 1775 as the most vicious and debilitating type of war.

Finally, we have Delaware's federal moment from the late 1780s to the 1820s. New Castle's renewed prosperity was found in its revived port, a complex of wharfs and docks that remained open well into the winter. Grass-roots political activity, lobbying the always difficult Delaware legislature, finally led to recognition in 1797 of a town government of Five Commissioners. At the same time, the Trustees of the Common sought permission to rent the Common so that funds could be raised for improvements in New Castle. In 1791, the Penn family approved the leasing policy, and the first tenant appeared six years later, after a battle with the Delaware legislature.

As a result of the passage of the federal Constitution, two political parties appeared, Federalist and Democratic-Republican. While in most states, the Federalist Party began to wane after the election of Thomas Jefferson as president in 1800, in Delaware the Federalists remained in power until the 1820s. The one place where the Democratic-Republicans showed strength was in New Castle and New Castle County. They maintained the earlier radical tradition of Revolutionary New Castle, as they favored the French Revolution, which the Federalists felt was too violent. The era culminated with the building of the Town Hall, a cooperative effort of the Trustees of the Common and the Five Commissioners and a symbol of hope for the future.

New Castle was a revolutionary community in the sense that it embraced radical politics, from Reverend Joseph Montgomery in 1775 to Archibald Alexander in 1794. As in any diverse community, there was always opposition to calm this ardor. While from 1774 to 1776 its Presbyterian meetinghouse took the lead in Delaware's Independence movement, its support of independence was counterbalanced by Immanuel Church and the Delaware Assembly. After the war, a healthy division of opinion existed on the direction of the new republic. New Castle came closer than anywhere in Delaware to fulfilling the ideals of Thomas Jefferson, the most radical of the Founding Fathers, with its Patriot Society. It made its mark on the wharfs of the port, in New Castle's Presbyterian meetinghouse and among the Five Commissioners of town government, which the events of the French Revolution inspired. New Castle was unique, ahead of the rest of Delaware, in the Presbyterian roots of its opposition to British government, in the firmness of its Independence movement and in its support of the liberty, equality and fraternity of the French Revolution.

Selected Bibliography

Primary

Booth, Elizabeth. *Reminiscences*. New Castle, DE: self-published, 1884.

Delaware Public Archives Commission. *Delaware Archive, Revolutionary War*. Wilmington, DE: Public Archives Commission of Delaware, 1911.

Dickinson, John. *Letters From a Farmer in Pennsylvania*. Englewood Cliffs, NJ: Prentice Hall, 1962.

Martin, James Kirby, ed. *Ordinary Courage: The Revolutionary Adventures of Joseph Plumb Martin*. St. James, NY: Brandywine Press, 1999.

McKean, Thomas. *A Calm Appeal to the People of Delaware*. Philadelphia, PA: Z. Poulson, 1793.

Minute Book Com's Town of New Castle. New Castle City Hall, 1797–1840.

Minutes of the Trustees of the Common. New Castle Town Hall, New Castle, 1791–1840.

Montgomery, Joseph. *A Sermon Produced at Christiana Bridge and New Castle*. Philadelphia, PA: Humphries, 1775.

Read, William T. *Life and Correspondence of George Read*. Philadelphia, PA: J.B. Lippincott and Company, 1870.

Records of the New Castle Presbyterian Church. Presbyterian Historical Society, Philadelphia, Pennsylvania.

Ryden, George H. *Letters to and from Caesar Rodney, 1756–1784*. Philadelphia, PA: Historical Society of Delaware, 1933.

Spotswood, J.B., Reverend. *Historical Sketch of the Presbyterian Church of New Castle, Delaware.* Philadelphia, PA: Joseph M. Wilson, Publisher, 1859.

Tilton, James. *Timoleon's Biographical History of Dionysius, Tyrant of Delaware.* Edited by John Munroe. Newark: University of Delaware Press, 1958.

SECONDARY

Alotta, Robert. *Another Part of the Field: America's Revolution 1777–78.* Shippensburg, PA: White Mane Publishing, 1991.

Bendler, Bruce. "Securing One of the Blessings of Liberty: Black Families in Lower New Castle County, 1790–1850," *Delaware History* 25 (Fall–Winter 1993–94): 237–52.

Bolster, W. Jeffrey. *Black Jacks: African American Seamen in the Age of Sail.* Cambridge, MA: Harvard University Press, 1997.

Coleman, John. *Thomas McKean: Forgotten Leader of the Revolution.* Rockaway, NJ: American Faculty Press, 1975.

Cooper, Constance. "A Town Among Cities: New Castle, Delaware, 1780–1840." Dissertation, University of Delaware, 1983.

Cooper, Constance, ed. *350 Years of New Castle, Delaware: Chapters in a Town's History.* Wilmington, DE: Cedar Tree Books, 2001.

Dalleo, Bruce, Peter Dalleo, Heidi Harendza and Catherine Hoffman Kaser. *Passing on the Story: African Americans in New Castle.* New Castle, DE: New Castle Historical Society, 2002.

Delaware Federal Writers' Project. *New Castle on the Delaware.* New Castle, DE: New Castle Historical Society, 1973.

Doerflinger, Thomas. *A Vigorous Spirit of Enterprise: Merchants and Economic Development in Revolutionary Philadelphia.* Chapel Hill: University of North Carolina Press, 1986.

Flower, Milton. *John Dickinson: Conservative Revolutionary.* Charlottesville: University Press of Virginia, 1983.

Foster, John Montgomery. *A Sketch of the Life of Rev. Joseph Montgomery.* Harrisburg, PA: privately published, 1879.

Gibson, George, ed. *The Collected Essays of Richard S. Rodney on Early Delaware.* Wilmington: Society of Colonial Wars in the State of Delaware, 1975.

Gillett, E.H. *History of the Presbyterian Church in the United States of America.* Philadelphia, PA: Presbyterian Board of Publication, 1864.

Gilmore, Peter. "The First Minister and the Second Sodom: Rev. Samuel Barr and the Social Origins of the Whiskey Rebellion." Paper delivered to the historical society of the First Presbyterian Church, Pittsburgh, Pennsylvania, May 2008.

Green, Stephen. "Understanding the Christian Nation Myth." *Cardozo L. Rev. de Novo* 245 (2010).

Hancock, Harold. "County Committees and the Growth of Independence in the Three Lower Counties on the Delaware, 1765–1776." *Delaware History* 15 (October 1973): 269–94.

———. "New Castle County Loyalists." *Delaware History* 4 (September 1951): 315–53.

Harding, Anneliese. *John Lewis Kimmel.* Winterthur, DE: Winterthur Press, 1994.

Hein, Kara, and Rebecca Siders. *A Documentary History of the Arsenal, New Castle, Delaware.* Newark: Center for Historic Architecture and Design, University of Delaware, 1998.

Heite, Louise, and Edward Heite. "Saving New Amstel: A Proposed City of New Castle Archeological Preservation Plan." Camden, Delaware, 1989.

Herman, Bernard. *The Stolen House.* Charlottesville: University Press of Virginia, 1992.

Hoffecker, Carol. *Democracy in Delaware: The Story of the First State's General Assembly.* Wilmington, DE: Cedar Tree Books, 2004.

Isaac, Rhys. *The Transformation of Virginia, 1740–1790.* Chapel Hill: University of North Carolina Press, 1982.

Kidd, Thomas. *God of Liberty: A Religious History of the American Revolution.* New York: Basic Books, 2010.

Lappen, James. *Presbyterians on Delmarva: The History of the New Castle Presbytery.* N.p.: self-published, 1972.

Main, Jackson Turner. *The Social Structure of Revolutionary America.* Princeton, NJ: Princeton University Press, 1965.

Miller, Kerby. *Emigrants and Exiles: Ireland and the Irish Exodus to North America.* New York: Oxford University Press, 1985.

Mullin, Timothy. "A Fresh Look at Old New Castle's Architectural Heritage." *Western Kentucky University Top Scholar.* Bowling Green: Western Kentucky University, 2007.

Munroe, John. *Colonial Delaware: A History.* Millwood, NY: KTO Press, 1978.

———. *Federalist Delaware, 1775–1815.* New Brunswick, NJ: Rutgers University Press, 1954.

New, M. Christopher. *Maryland Loyalists in the American Revolution.* Centreville, MD: Tidewater Publishers, 1996.

New Castle Community History and Archaeology Project. New Castle, Delaware, nc-chap.org.

New Castle Presbyterian History Committee. *Time-Line of New Castle Presbyterian Church.* New Castle, DE: self-distributed, 2011.

Peare, Catherine. *William Penn: A Biography.* Philadelphia, PA: Lippincott Company, 1956.

Pougher, Richard. "'Averse…to Remaining Idle Spectators': The Emergence of Loyalist Privateering during the American Revolution." PhD thesis, University of Maine, 2002.

Rightmyer, Nelson. *The Anglican Church in Delaware.* Philadelphia, PA: The Church Historical Society, 1947.

Riordan, Liam. *Many Identities, One Nation: The Revolution and Its Legacy in the Mid-Atlantic.* Philadelphia: University of Pennsylvania Press, 2007.

Rosswurm, Steven. *Arms, Country and Class: The Philadelphia Militia and the "Lower Sort" during the American Revolution.* New Brunswick, NJ: Rutgers University Press, 1989.

Rowe, G.S. *Thomas McKean: The Shaping of an American Republicanism.* Boulder: University of Colorado Press, 1978.

Smith, Abbot. *Colonists in Bondage: White Servitude and Convict Labor in America 1607–1776.* New York: W.W. Norton, 1971.

Tait, L. Gordon. *The Piety of John Witherspoon: Pew, Pulpit and Public Forum.* Louisville, KY: Geneva Press, 2001.

Truitt, Charles. *Breadbasket of the Revolution: Delmarva's Eight Turbulent War Years.* Baltimore, MD: Publication Press, 1975.

Trustees of the New Castle Common. *New Castle Common.* Wilmington, DE: self-published, 1944.

Ward, Christopher. *The Delaware Continentals, 1776–1783.* Wilmington: Historical Society of Delaware, 1941.

———. *The War of the Revolution.* New York: Macmillan Company, 1952.

Waterson, Elizabeth. *Churches in Delaware during the Revolution.* Wilmington: Historical Society of Delaware, 1925.

Index

A

Act of Free Pardon and Oblivion 69
Admiralty Court of Delaware in New Castle 48, 79, 116
African American 22, 86, 99, 100
Alexander, Archibald 90, 95, 98, 103, 106, 107, 108, 109, 117
Alison, Francis 35, 36, 40, 49
Almond, William 70
Anglicans 25, 31, 34, 37, 42, 44, 46, 47, 48, 50, 64, 68, 82, 83, 86
Appleton, Robert 79
Appoquinimy Church 32, 33
Armitage, Sally 36, 41
Armstrong, James 45, 46
Asbury, John 86
Aull, John 91
Aull, William 91, 103

B

Baltimore 59, 77, 90, 91
Baptists 44, 45, 83, 86
Barr, Samuel 83
Bedford, Gunning, Sr. 7, 22, 57, 63, 64, 98, 102, 105, 106
Bethany United African Methodist Church 84, 100
Bible Society of Delaware 84, 87
Black, James 61
Blanc, Ives 90
Boggs, Joseph 98
Bond, Thomas 90, 91
Booth, Ann Clay 49, 87
Booth, James 15, 27, 48, 75, 87, 90, 98, 103, 105
Booth, Joseph 60
Brandywine, Battle of the 60, 62, 69, 115
Brewster, John 31
British Constitution 22, 29, 40, 105
British Isles 20, 24, 27, 34, 35, 37, 48, 51, 73, 96

C

Cantwell, Richard 59
Chester County, PA 20
Chestertown, MD 77
Chow, Cheney 72
Christiana River 19, 33
  Christiana Bridge 33, 46, 52, 83
  Head of Christiana 32, 45
Church of Scotland 34, 35, 37
Clark, John 59
Clay, Robert 85
Clay, Slator 20
Cloud's Row 20
Colesbery, Jacob 15
College of New Jersey (Princeton) 37, 44, 45, 46, 83
College of Philadelphia 36, 45, 63, 82, 96
Common 12, 15, 17, 25, 26, 27, 81, 93, 95, 96, 98, 113, 116

Congregational Church 34
Conner, Isaac 70
Continental army 44, 60, 63, 72, 73, 76, 77, 78
Continental Congress 37, 38, 39, 40, 42, 49, 53, 56
Cooch's Bridge, Battle of 56, 59, 60, 69, 115
Cornwallis, Charles 77, 78
Cornwallis, William 78
county lot 13, 17
Court of Common Pleas 36, 42, 107
Crowding, Peter 96, 108
Crow, John 103

D

Declaration of Independence 17, 20, 25, 37, 39, 40, 48, 54, 55, 56, 63, 115
deism 35
Delany, Peter 113
Delaware Constitutional Conventions 48
Delaware Continentals 44, 64
Delaware Council of Safety 57
Delaware Legislative Council 55, 71, 98
Delaware Privy Council 55, 61, 102
Delaware River 24, 27, 34, 42, 65, 66, 67, 71, 72, 75, 77, 78, 79, 116
Delaware Society for Promoting the Abolition of Slavery 99
Delaware Whig Battalion 61
Democratic-Republicans 105, 106, 107, 108, 111, 116
Derickson, Jacob 58
Dickinson, John 27, 28, 29, 35, 38, 39, 51, 55, 56, 77, 98, 101, 104
Douglas, Andrew Snape 75
Dover (Kent County) 17, 54, 56, 61, 75, 77, 94, 99, 102, 116
Drake, John 69, 74
Drawyers Church 32, 33
Duck Creek 61, 75, 79
Duff, Thomas 59
Duke of York 12
Dunmore, Governor 73, 74
Dutch 11, 12, 22, 24
Dutch Reformed Church 31, 46

E

Elizabethan Compromise 34
Enlightenment 27, 35, 36, 37, 46, 81, 83, 92, 96, 110

F

Farmer's Bank of Delaware 111
federal Constitutions 94, 98, 102, 104, 116
Federalists 104, 105, 106, 107, 108, 109, 111, 116
Ferguson, Patrick 69
Finney, David 20, 40, 41, 98
Finney, John 20, 41
Five Commissioners, the 13, 91, 103, 104, 107, 113, 116, 117
Flying Camp 60, 62, 64
forts
- Mercer 67, 75
- Mifflin 67, 75
- Red Bank 67

Frank Leslie's Illustrated Newspaper as *Relic of Barbarism* 110
French Revolution 83, 116, 117
Frenchtown, MD 90, 91

G

galleys 67, 73, 74, 75
Galloway, George 55
Germain, George 71, 73
Germantown, Battle of 62
Glorious Revolution 24, 27, 34
Green, the 12, 13, 15, 17, 18, 27, 46, 63, 86, 96, 110, 115
Greenwood, John 70

H

Hackett, Abraham 70
Hair, John 96
Hall, David 62, 64, 82, 109
Hamilton, Alexander 105
Hamond, Andrew Snape 73, 74, 75
Hancock, John 37

Haslet, John 39, 44, 59, 62, 63, 64, 82
Haslet, Joseph 109
Hazelwood, John 67
Head of Elk 56, 65, 69, 78
HMS *Iris* 75, 78
HMS *Lady's Revenge* 79
HMS *Liverpool* 73, 74
HMS *Medea* 78
HMS *Pearl* 75
HMS *Roebuck* 69, 73, 74, 75
Howe, William 46, 55, 56, 59, 60, 61, 63, 65, 67, 68, 69, 72, 74, 78, 115
Huguenots 24
Hundreds
  Brandywine 19, 33, 58, 61
  Christiana 19, 33, 45, 53, 96
  Dover 25, 52
  New Castle 19, 23, 26, 27, 53, 63, 70, 79, 81, 86, 93, 104
  Pencader 19, 33, 86
  Red Lion 19, 42, 108
  St. George's 19, 25, 33, 45, 96
  White Clay Creek 19, 33
Hutcheson, Francis 36, 37

I

Immanuel Church 12, 15, 25, 46, 48, 49, 85, 98, 117
Intolerable Acts 13, 45, 52

J

James, John 61, 102
Janvier, John 90
Janvier, Thomas 31
Jaquett, Peter 82, 83, 106
Jefferson, Thomas 92, 97, 105, 107, 108, 116, 117
Jones, Roger 78

K

Kelsey, William 17
Kent County, DE 27, 48, 53, 56, 59, 62, 66, 77, 82, 86, 101
Killen, William 39
Kimmel, John Lewis 22
Knyphausen, Wilhelm 69

L

Latimer, James 33, 34, 57, 102
Latrobe, Benjamin 13, 15, 97, 99, 103
Latrobe map 11, 90
Latta, John Ewing 83, 84, 87
Lewes (Sussex County) 44, 55, 72, 74, 76, 78
Lewis, Isaac 61, 75
Lexington and Concord, Battles of 38, 43, 53
Livingston, Robert (Essay on Sheep) 92
Livingston, William 72, 76
Long Hook (New Castle County) 82
Long Island and White Plains, Battles of 60
Lower Counties Assembly 11, 17, 20
loyalists 46, 48, 50, 54, 55, 58, 61, 62, 64, 68, 69, 70, 71, 72, 73, 76, 77, 79, 82, 86, 105, 116
Loyalist Test Act 82
Lutherans 31, 64

M

Madison, James 85
Manlove, Boaz 54
manumission 23, 99
Market House 7, 10, 11, 18, 26, 27
Market Trustees 11, 103
Martin, Joseph Plumb 67
Maryland 19, 20, 22, 24, 44, 48, 49, 50, 52, 56, 60, 61, 65, 66, 72, 75, 77, 101, 106
Mason, John 102
Maurice, Theodore 49, 63, 68
Maxwell, William 59, 69
McCallmont, Charles and Susanna 108
McCreary, John 45
McKean, Dorthe 42
McKean, Thomas 20, 25, 27, 36, 38, 39, 40, 41, 44, 49, 51, 52, 53, 54, 56, 59, 60, 61, 64, 68, 75, 94, 95, 98, 104
McKinly, John 39, 68, 74
McLane, Allen 79
McLonen, Daniel 20
McWilliam, Richard 20, 41, 54
Mennonites 68
Mercer, Hugh 60
Methodists 44, 45, 64, 79, 84, 86, 99, 100

Monroe, John 39, 40
Montgomery, James 76
Montgomery, Joseph 41, 43, 44, 45, 46, 50, 59, 63, 117
Montgomery, Rachel Rush 44, 59
Moody, William 61
Morrison, Robert 20
Munro, George 20, 53, 92, 95, 99, 109
Munro, Jemma Haslet 96

N

Navigation Acts 51
New Castle Academy 84, 96
New Castle County Agricultural Association 92
New Castle County Committee 17
New Castle County Committee of Correspondence 52
New Castle County Committee of Inspection 42
New Castle County Grand Jury 52, 53
New Castle County militia 34, 48, 56, 58, 59, 60, 63, 69
New Castle Courthouse 53
New Castle Library Company 92
New Castle Presbyterian meetinghouse 32
New Castle Presbytery 32, 35, 45, 46, 83
New Castle Town Hall 111
New Castle Turnpike Company 108
New London Academy, PA 36
Newport, DE 33, 53, 72, 102
New York City 55
Nicholson, James 77
Nodes, Thomas 70
North, Joshua 58
Nova Scotia 70

O

Oxford, MD 77

P

Palatines 24
Parliament 13, 18, 27, 28, 29, 34, 35, 39, 47, 51, 52
Patriotic Society of New Castle County 106
Patterson, Samuel 49, 53, 58, 59, 60, 61
Peace of Paris 70, 79, 94
Pearce, Matthew 98
Penn, Richard 16, 20, 22, 68
Pennsylvania navy 67
Penn, Thomas 16, 20, 22
Penn, William 12, 15, 17, 19, 20, 22, 25, 54, 68, 94, 96
Philadelphia 17, 19, 22, 23, 24, 33, 34, 35, 37, 38, 39, 40, 49, 51, 52, 56, 59, 60, 61, 65, 66, 69, 72, 75, 76, 77, 78, 82, 88, 90, 92, 96, 100, 101, 108, 111, 115, 116
Philadelphia Committee of Correspondence 13
Physick, Edmund 94
picaroons 72, 78, 79
pirates 72, 73, 79
Porter, Alexander 42
Presbyterian General Assembly 84
Presbyterians 25, 32, 34, 35, 38, 40, 45, 46, 47, 48, 68, 103, 106
  New Light 44, 45
  Old Light 45, 83, 85
Presbyterian Synod 37, 38, 39, 44, 116

Q

Quakers 23, 31, 44, 68
Queen Anne 47, 72

R

Rankin, William 61
Read, George, Jr. 15, 98, 103, 108, 111
Read, George, Sr. 20, 22, 25, 27, 36, 38, 44, 48, 49, 53, 54, 55, 57, 63, 66, 68, 71, 82, 83, 85, 98, 101, 102, 105, 106
Read, Gertrude Ross 49, 50
Read, William and Sally 108
refugees 72, 73, 75, 76, 77, 78, 79
Reid, Thomas 37
Revolutionary War 5, 13, 22, 34, 39, 46, 49, 81, 86, 93, 98, 99, 106

Riddle, James 15, 90, 92, 98, 106
Robinson, Thomas 54
Rodney, Caesar 49, 53, 56, 59, 62, 64, 73, 75, 78
Rodney, George 76
Rodney, Thomas 77, 78
Ross, Aeneas 48, 50
Ross, George 25, 46, 47, 49
Royal Navy 47, 65, 66, 67, 68, 69, 70, 71, 72, 73, 75, 78, 106, 115, 116
Rumsey, John 108
Rush, Benjamin 37, 41, 59, 63, 64

S

Schuyler, Philip 63
Scots-Irish 24, 25, 32, 33, 35, 37, 40, 42, 46, 61, 62, 87
Serle, Ambrose 67, 68
Silsbee, John 98
Silsbee, Nathaniel 20
Slater, Thomas 72
Smallwood, William 50
Smith, Christian 70
Snow, Silas 75
Society for the Propagation of the Gospel 47
Spencer, Elihu 45
Spencer, Peter 100
Stamp Act 27, 28, 29, 36, 40, 45, 51, 52
Stockton, John 98
Stonum 25, 71
St. Peters Roman Catholic Church 87
streets
  Delaware 11, 15, 48, 86
  Front 25, 31, 63, 90, 91
  Market 11, 12
  Second 91
  Third 12
Sussex County, DE 42, 54, 55, 56, 61, 72, 76

T

Thomas, Charles 108, 109, 110, 111
Thomas, Eliza Stoops 108
Thompson, John 41, 42
Throne, Sydenhame 48
Tilton, James 82, 83, 106
Townshend Duties 27, 28, 52
Trinity 55
Trustees of the Common 5, 15, 16, 18, 20, 26, 94, 95, 96, 98, 103, 104, 105, 111, 113, 116
Turner, Thomas 113

U

Ulster 33, 35, 45, 59, 62, 83, 91, 106
Union Fire Company 18
University of Edinburgh 37
University of Glasgow 35, 36, 83
USS *Confederacy* 75
USS *General Greene* 76
USS *Hancock* 78
USS *Trumbull* 77, 78

V

Van Gezell, John 20
Van Leuvenigh 20, 44, 88
Virginia 19, 20, 22, 24, 48, 52, 60, 63, 73, 74, 75, 76, 77, 83, 91, 96, 106, 109

W

Washington, George 34, 44, 55, 59, 60, 62, 64, 72, 76, 77, 78, 79, 104, 105, 115
Watson, John 68, 69, 72
Watson's Loyalist Association 69
Watson, Thomas 61
Welsh Tract 32, 33, 86
West Indies 34, 51, 78, 82, 90
Wharton, Charles 50
Whitefield, George 35, 45, 46
William and Mary 27, 34
Wilmington 11, 33, 49, 66, 78, 86, 90, 96, 99, 100, 108
Wilson, Christopher 70
Wilson, John 31, 33
Witherspoon, John 35, 37, 38, 39, 44

Y

Yeates, John 20
Yorktown, siege of 62, 78, 79, 81

About the Author

Historian Theodore Corbett has also authored *The Clash of Cultures on the Warpath of Nations: The Colonial Wars in the Hudson-Champlain Valley* (2002); *The Making of American Resorts: Saratoga Springs, Ballston Spa and Lake George* (2001); and the forthcoming *The Saratoga Campaign: Civil War Denies the Fruits of Victory*. He lives in New Castle's historic district with his wife, Christine, and they own Historic Village Quilts, a shop on Delaware Street.